NUTCASES

CRIMINAL LAW

Other Titles in the Series

Constitutional and Administrative Law
Contract Law
Criminal Law
European Union Law
Employment Law
Equity and Trusts
Human Rights
Land Law
Tort

Titles in the Nutshell Series

A Level Law
Company Law
Consumer Law
Contract Law
Constitutional and Administrative Law
Criminal Law
Employment Law
English Legal System
Environmental Law
European Union Law
Equity and Trusts
Evidence
Family Law
Human Rights
Intellectual Property Law
Land Law
Medical Law
Tort
Trusts

AUSTRALIA
Law Book Company
Sydney

CANADA and USA
Carswell
Toronto

HONG KONG
Sweet & Maxwell Asia

NEW ZEALAND
Brookers
Wellington

SINGAPORE and MALAYSIA
Sweet & Maxwell Asia
Singapore and Kuala Lumpur

NUTCASES

CRIMINAL LAW

FOURTH EDITION

by

PENNY CHILDS, LL.B., LL.M.
Senior Lecturer in Law
University of Plymouth

London • Sweet & Maxwell • 2005

Published in 2005 by Sweet & Maxwell Limited of
100 Avenue Road, London NW3 3PF
Typeset by LBJ Typesetting Ltd
Printed in Great Britain by Creative Print & Design

No natural forests were destroyed to make this product.
Only farmed timber was used and re-planted.

A CIP catalogue record for this book is available
from the British Library.

ISBN 0421 89010X

CONTENTS

TABLE OF CASES

1. ACTUS REUS

Acts and Omissions

Key Principle: **The definition of some offences is restricted to liability for acts. In such cases, an omission is insufficient unless it can be construed as an act.**

Fagan v Metropolitan Police Commissioner 1969
The defendant drove his car onto a policeman's foot. This may have been accidental but then he deliberately refused to move. He claimed that the original act was not assault because he lacked *mens rea* and the rest of his conduct was an omission which could not amount to assault.

Held: (DC) Defendant's appeal dismissed. Assault cannot be committed by omission. However, the assault was not complete on mounting the foot but continued until the car was removed. Therefore, failing to remove the car was not a mere omission but was part of a continuing act. [1969] 1 Q.B. 439

Commentary
Assault is one offence that cannot be committed by omission. Others include burglary, robbery, attempt and constructive manslaughter. Fagan would have been acquitted if his conduct could only be described as an omission. For other examples of the consequences and difficulties involved in categorising conduct, see *R. v Miller* (1983) (see p.3) and *Airedale NHS Trust v Bland* (1993) (see p.4).

Key Principle: **Where an *actus reus* can be committed by omission, a defendant who fails to act is only liable if under a duty to act.**

Key Principle: **A duty to act may arise through contract.**

R. v Instan 1893
The defendant lived with her aged aunt who died after the defendant failed to feed her or get medical help when she became unable to care for herself.

Held: (CCCR) Conviction for manslaughter upheld. The defendant was under a duty because food was paid for by the aunt, who relied on the niece as her only source of maintenance. [1893] 1 Q.B. 450

Commentary
A common law duty could arise from the familial relationship, but it is doubtful whether such a duty arises where the parties are of full age and capacity. It could also arise because the aunt depended on the niece, who had voluntarily assumed a duty. Moreover, the court felt that the duty could arise from a contract, implied from the circumstances of the case.

R. v Pittwood 1902
A railway gate-keeper, whose duties involved shutting a gate when trains passed, forgot to shut the gate. A person crossing the track was killed by an oncoming train.

Held: (Assize Ct) The defendant was guilty of manslaughter due to the duty imposed by his contract of employment. It did not matter that the contract was between him and a third party (his employers). (1902) 19 T.L.R. 37

Key Principle: **A duty to act may arise from the close relationship between defendant and victim.**

R. v Gibbins & Proctor 1918
A father and his common law wife failed to feed his child who died as a result. They were convicted of murder.

Held: (CA) Defendant's appeal dismissed. The father was guilty of murder, having breached the duty owed by parents to their children. (1918) 13 Cr.App.R. 134

Commentary
Duties can also be imposed by statute. The duty in this case could today also arise as a statutory duty under the *Children and Young Persons Act 1933*.

Key Principle: **A common law duty to act may arise through the voluntary assumption of care.**

R. v Stone & Dobinson 1977
An aged woman lived with her brother (Stone) and his common law wife (Dobinson). She refused to eat and became seriously ill and bedridden. For a number of reasons, the defendants failed to summon medical help and the sister eventually died.

Held: (CA) Appeal against conviction for manslaughter dismissed. The jury was entitled to decide that the defendants owed a duty to get help or to care for the deceased once she became helplessly infirm. The assumption of a duty could be inferred from the facts that both defendants were aware of her condition; she was a blood relation of Stone, living in his house; and Dobinson had undertaken the duty of trying to wash and feed her. [1977] Q.B. 354

Commentary

(1) Reference to Stone's relationship with the deceased suggests a common law duty based on special relationship but it is unlikely that a duty would have been owed if she had not been living in his home. There was no such relationship with Dobinson but she had apparently assumed a duty by trying to care for the deceased. Does this mean that Dobinson would have been under no duty if she had not acted at all? What about Stone?

(2) Other cases falling within this category are *Instan* and the common law wife's duty in *Gibbins & Proctor*.

Key Principle: **A common law duty to act may arise from creating a dangerous situation.**

R. v Miller 1983
The defendant accidentally set fire to a mattress by falling asleep with a lighted cigarette. When he awoke, he failed to take any steps to extinguish the fire or prevent further damage.

Held: (HL) Appeal against conviction for arson dismissed. Arson can be committed by act or omission. Where defendants create a dangerous situation and it is within their power to counteract that danger, a responsibility arises to do so. Since the defendant could, without danger or difficulty, have minimised the risk he had created, his failure to do so amounted to arson. [1983] A.C. 161

Commentary

(1) The case deals with the *Criminal Damage Act 1971* but is presumably of more general application (although it may be restricted to result crimes). For example, in a case on manslaughter, *R. v Khan (Rungzabe and Tahir)* (1998) (CA), a duty to call medical help was capable of arising where the defendants had supplied the victim with heroin and failed to act when she became comatose.

(2) The duty is simply to take reasonable steps (safely open to the defendant) and only arose because the defendant created the danger in the first place. Lord Diplock contrasted the case of a passive bystander who sees a fire but is under no duty to act.

Key Principle: **A person may be discharged from their duty to act, incurring no liability for an omission thereafter.**

Airedale NHS Trust v Bland 1993
A patient had been in a persistent vegetative state for over three years. The doctors and family wanted to withdraw treatment and artificial feeding and the health authority successfully applied for a court order to do so. The Official Solicitor appealed on the basis that withdrawal breached the doctor's duty to the patient.

Held: (HL) Appeal dismissed. In light of the patient's condition and views of the medical personnel, the declaration was granted. Whilst a doctor was under a duty to act in the best interests of a patient, continuation of treatment was not always in those best interests. In this case, since there was no chance of recovery, withdrawing treatment would not breach the doctor's duty. [1993] A.C. 789

Commentary
The case further illustrates the difficulties involved in classifying conduct as an act or omission. The court stated that it was always unlawful to take positive steps to end a patient's life. It was only where the case was one of omission that it might be lawful because no duty was breached. This means that liability turns on how the conduct is classified: is withdrawing treatment an act or an omission?

States of Affairs

Key Principle: **Conduct must generally be voluntary. However, voluntariness may not be required where the *actus reus* consists of a state of affairs (or event) rather than conduct.**

R. v Larsonneur 1933
A Frenchwoman, required to leave the UK, did so by going to Eire. She was deported from Eire and handed to the police in the UK. She was convicted of "being an alien . . . found in the UK" (without leave) and appealed on the basis that her return was caused by circumstances over which she had no control.

Held: (CA) Appeal dismissed. The defendant was found in the UK after expiration of permission to be there and so had violated the conditions of her passport. (1933) 24 Cr.App.R. 74

Commentary
The case has been criticised since the defendant's presence was involuntary. However, the cause of the prohibited state of affairs was apparently irrelevant. A similar decision was reached in *Winzar* (1983), where the defendant was guilty of "being found drunk . . . on a highway", having been placed there by the police.

Unlawfulness

Key Principle: **The word "unlawful" may be included as part of the *actus reus* of a crime.**

R. v Williams (Gladstone) 1984
The defendant punched the victim mistakenly believing that the victim was unlawfully assaulting another. He was convicted of assault occasioning actual bodily harm and appealed against the

direction that his honest belief that he was acting lawfully was only relevant if based on reasonable grounds. Whether this was a misdirection depended on whether the word "unlawful" was a matter of defence or part of the *actus reus* of the offence (see Ch.2).

Held: (CA) Appeal allowed for reasons explained in Ch.2. The word "unlawful" was part of the *actus reus* of assault, with the prosecution bearing the burden of proving that the actions were unlawful. Therefore the defendant had made a mistake about an element appearing in the *actus reus* of the crime charged. (1984) 78 Cr.App.R. 276

Commentary
In *Albert v Lavin* (1981) (see Ch.2, p.25), the Divisional Court held that "unlawfulness" was a defence issue and not part of the definition of assault. However, the Court of Appeal in *R. v Kimber* (1983) (see Ch.2, p.23), disagreed. The court in *Williams* expressly disapproved *Albert v Lavin* and confirmed *Kimber* (1983). This was further approved by the Privy Council in *Beckford v R.* (1988) (see Ch.14, p.167).

Causation—In Fact

Key Principle: **Causation in fact requires that the defendant's conduct be a *sine qua non* ("but-for" cause) of a result.**

R. v White 1910
The defendant was charged with murder having put cyanide into his mother's drink with intention to kill her. Medical evidence established that her death was due to heart failure and not the poison.

Held: (CA) The defendant was not guilty of murder, but he was, on the evidence, guilty of attempted murder. [1910] 2 K.B. 124

Commentary
Whilst the decision (concerned with attempted murder) does not deal directly with the point, it is a good illustration of lack of factual causation. But for his act, the defendant's mother would still have died and so he was not the *sine qua non* (cause) of her death.

Causation—In Law

Key Principle: **The defendant's conduct does not have to be the sole (or main) cause of a result but it must more than minimally contribute to it.**

R. v Pagett 1983
The defendant held a woman in front of him as he fired at armed police. The police returned fire, killing the woman. The defendant appealed against conviction on two grounds:

(1) the immediate cause of the death was the act of the police and not attributable to the defendant.

(2) the judge had misdirected the jury in saying that causation was matter of law rather than fact.

Held: (CA) Appeal dismissed.

(1) The defendant had caused the death despite the actions of the police. A defendant "need not be the sole cause or even the main cause . . . it being enough that his act contributed significantly".

(2) Causation is a question for the jury to decide on the facts but must be decided in accordance with legal principles. (1983) 76 Cr.App.R. 279

Key Principle: **If an event intervenes between the defendant's conduct and the result, it may be a *novus actus interveniens* (a new operative cause), breaking the chain of causation.**

R. v Jordan 1956
The defendant stabbed the victim who died a few days later following treatment for the wound. The wound had almost healed and the immediate cause of death was the medical treatment, described as "palpably wrong". The defendant appealed against conviction for murder.

Held: (CA) Conviction quashed. The direct and immediate cause of death was a separate and independent feature (the treatment) and not the stab wound. (1956) 40 Cr.App.R. 152

Commentary
It was suggested that where death arose from normal treatment for an injury, the injury could be said to be a cause of death. However, this treatment was not normal and so broke the chain.

Key Principle: **An intervening event will not break the chain of causation if the defendant's conduct is still an operative and substantial cause of the result.**

R. v Smith 1959
The defendant stabbed the victim, causing internal injury. A medical officer, not realising the nature of the injury, gave "thoroughly bad" treatment. The victim died within two hours of being stabbed but might not have died if given different treatment. The defendant appealed against conviction for murder on the basis that the treatment broke the chain.

Held: (CMAC) Appeal dismissed. Death resulted from the original wound which was still an operating and substantial cause of the death despite other operative causes. [1959] 2 Q.B. 35

Commentary
The court distinguished *Jordan* as "a very particular case, depending on its exact facts". *Jordan* was also said to be "very exceptional" (and *Smith* was preferred) in *Malcherek & Steel* (1981) (CA) where life support for two injured victims was disconnected by doctors. Since the treatment was "normal and conventional" and the original injuries were still operative, the court held that discontinuing treatment did not break the chain of causation. Also, note the view in *Airedale* that allowing a patient to die of a pre-existing condition does not, in law, amount to causing the death which is still treated as caused by the pre-existing condition. Overall, the distinction between *Smith* and *Jordan* seems to be that in *Jordan* the wound, having practically healed, ceased to operate. Any attempt to distinguish the cases on the degree of fault involved in the treatment should now be avoided according to *R. v Cheshire* (1991) (see below).

Key Principle: **To operate as a *novus actus interveniens,* the**

intervening event must be so potent and independent of the defendant's actions as to render those actions "insignificant".

R. v Cheshire 1991
The defendant shot the victim in the abdomen and thigh. The victim developed breathing difficulties, necessitating a tracheotomy. Two months after the shooting, the wounds had practically healed but the victim died from complications caused by the tracheotomy. The defendant was convicted of murder and appealed against the direction that only grossly negligent or reckless treatment broke the chain of causation.

Held: (CA) Appeal dismissed. It was a misdirection to focus on the degree of fault involved in the medical treatment but no miscarriage of justice had occurred. The complication from which the victim died was a direct consequence of the defendant's conduct which was still a significant cause of the death. This was not an extraordinary or unusual case where treatment was so independent of the defendant's conduct and so potent in causing death as to exonerate the defendant. [1991] 3 All E.R. 670

Commentary
Factually, the case is similar to *Jordan* since the original wound had ceased to operate. However, only treatment that is so extraordinary as to be independent of the defendant's conduct breaks the chain and *obiter* in *Cheshire* suggests that incompetence does not of itself render treatment "abnormal in the sense of extraordinary".

Key Principle: **An intervening act will not break the chain of causation if it is dependent on the defendant's conduct and not a free (voluntary) act.**

R. v Pagett 1983
(see p.7).

Held: (CA) In dismissing the defendant's appeal, the court stated that an intervention must be independent and voluntary ("free, deliberate and informed") to break the chain. A reasonable act of self-defence or self-preservation (such as the police returning fire) did not break the chain because it was an involuntary response, dependent on the defendant's actions. For the same reason, an act carried out in the execution of a legal duty (such as preventing a crime or effecting an arrest) would not operate as a *novus actus*. (1983) 76 Cr.App.R. 279

Commentary

Further illustrations of the principle that an independent and voluntary act will break the chain of causation have arisen in a number of recent "death by drugs" cases. These cases have considered the liability of drug suppliers following the voluntary self-administration of drugs by users. In *R. v Kennedy* (1999) the defendant supplied the user with a syringe of prepared heroin. He was found guilty of manslaughter when the user died despite the "free, deliberate and informed" intervention of the user in injecting the drug. The reasoning in *Kennedy* is doubtful for a number of reasons and is distinguished in the case of *R. v Dias* (2002). In *Dias*, the Court of Appeal took the view that self-injection by the user might break the chain of causation and allowed the defendant's appeal in similar circumstances to those in *Kennedy*.

For other cases dealing with a similar point, see *R. v Rogers* (2003) and *R. v Finlay* (2003).

Key Principle: **An attempt by the victim to escape from the defendant's conduct will not break the chain of causation if it is reasonably foreseeable.**

R. v Williams & Davis 1992

A hitch-hiker jumped from a moving car and died from the injuries sustained. The victim had, according to the prosecution, jumped to escape violence from the defendants who intended to rob him.

Held: (CA) Appeal against conviction for manslaughter allowed. An attempt to escape from a threat does not break the chain if it is within the range of responses which could be foreseen by the reasonable person. However, in this case, there was insufficient evidence about the nature of the threat to determine whether or not the hitch-hiker's response was reasonable. [1992] 2 All E.R. 183

Commentary

The case confirms the conditions applying to escape attempts: the defendant caused the victim immediate fear of being hurt; the fear was well-founded and caused the escape attempt in the course of which the injury was sustained; the response was a natural consequence of the defendant's action (*i.e.* reasonably foreseeable as likely to happen, bearing in mind the agony of the moment and any particular characteristics of the victim). Compare the decision with *R. v Roberts* (1971) (see Ch.4, p.42) where there was sufficient evidence to suggest that the victim's response was reasonably foreseeable rather than "daft" or unexpected.

Key Principle: **An "abnormality" in the victim will not break the chain of causation, even if it is not reasonably foreseeable.**

R. v Blaue 1975
The defendant stabbed the victim who died after refusing a blood transfusion because she was a Jehovah's witness. The defendant appealed against conviction for manslaughter on the basis that the victim's refusal broke the chain.

Held: (CA) Appeal dismissed. The operative cause of the victim's death was the stab wound and not her refusal of treatment. The chain was not broken by the refusal because "people must take their victims as they find them". [1975] 3 All E.R. 446

Commentary
The rule, stated *obiter*, that victims be taken as found (which covers physical and other attributes) prevents a break in the chain even though it may be an unforeseeable "abnormality".

Key Principle: **If the defendant commits a number of different acts and the prosecution cannot prove which one caused the specified result, the defendant must be acquitted unless *mens rea* accompanied each of the acts that may have caused the result.**

Attorney-General's Reference (No.4 of 1980) 1981
The defendant slapped the victim, causing her to fall downstairs and bang her head. He dragged her upstairs by a piece of rope tied around her neck, cut her throat, dismembered her body and

disposed of the pieces. The prosecution could not prove which act caused her death and the judge directed an acquittal.

Held: (CA) It was not necessary to prove which act caused death as long as the jury was satisfied that each possible cause was accompanied by the relevant *mens rea*. However, if the jury felt that any one of the relevant acts was not accompanied by *mens rea*, they must acquit even where satisfied that the remaining acts were so accompanied. [1981] 2 All E.R. 617

Commentary
A conviction for manslaughter was possible because evidence suggested that all of the acts were accompanied by the *mens rea* of manslaughter. Contrast *Fisher* (1987) (CA) where the prosecution could not prove whether death was caused by hitting the victim or by dragging him downstairs. The defendant was acquitted because whilst the dragging was accompanied by *mens rea*, the blow may have been in self-defence.

Contemporaneity

Key Principle: **The *actus reus* and *mens rea* of a crime must be contemporaneous (coincide in time). Where an *actus reus* initially occurs without *mens rea*, contemporaneity may be achieved if the *actus reus* is construed as a continuing act and *mens rea* occurs during its continuance.**

Fagan v Metropolitan Police Commissioner 1969
(see p.1).

Held: (DC) Appeal dismissed. The court confirmed that "... both ... *actus reus* and *mens rea* must be present at the same time". However, lack of contemporaneity was avoided by construing the *actus reus* as continuing from its inception (when there was no *mens rea*) until the car was removed (when there was *mens rea*). [1969] 1 Q.B. 439

Commentary
For another illustration of this principle, see *Kaitamaki v R.* (1985) (Ch.5, p.46). A similar problem arose in *Miller* (1983) where the act of starting the fire was not accompanied by *mens rea*. *Mens rea* was formed later when the defendant failed to act. The Court of

Appeal adopted the approach in *Fagan*, treating the conduct as a continuing act so that *mens rea* was formed during its continuance. The House of Lords rejected this approach, deciding that the conduct was an omission and not a continuing act. They achieved the same result by holding that the failure to act (accompanied by *mens rea*) was the *actus reus*. This approach is only possible where the offence can be committed by omission and there is a duty to act.

Key Principle: **Where a series of acts culminate in the *actus reus*, and *mens rea* existed before but not at the time of the *actus reus*, contemporaneity is achieved if the series of acts are a continuous transaction connecting *actus reus* and *mens rea*.**

Thabo Meli v R. 1954

In pursuance of a pre-conceived plan to kill and evade detection, the defendants assaulted the victim. Believing him to be dead, they "staged" an accident by dropping the body over a cliff where the victim ultimately died from exposure.

Held: (PC) Defendant's appeal against conviction for murder dismissed. The first act(s), done with *mens rea*, did not cause death and the act(s) which did cause death were not accompanied by *mens rea*. However, the acts were not separate. They were all part of the plan and therefore represented one series of acts during which *actus reus* and *mens rea* were present. [1954] 1 All E.R. 373

R. v Church 1966

The defendant was convicted of manslaughter, having assaulted the victim with intent. Apparently believing the victim to be dead, he threw her body in a river where she died from drowning.

Held: (CA) Defendant's appeal dismissed. The jury was entitled to treat the series of acts as one course of conduct. Therefore, because the first act would establish (at least) manslaughter if the victim had died, the defendant was guilty even though he lacked *mens rea* at the time of doing the act that caused death. [1966] 1 Q.B. 59

Commentary

(1) The court also felt that murder was possible if the series of acts were designed to cause death or grievous bodily harm.

(2) There was no pre-conceived plan as in *Thabo Meli* (1954) nor did the court explain why, in the absence of such, this could still be viewed as one transaction. Explanation comes in the next case.

R. v Le Brun 1992
In the course of an argument, the defendant hit his wife, causing her to become unconscious. In dragging her away thereafter, he caused her death by accidentally dropping her body. He was convicted of manslaughter.

Held: (CA) Defendant's appeal dismissed. Where there is a time interval between the act done with *mens rea* (the original assault) and the act that causes death, there may still be a conviction if all the acts are part of the same sequence of events (the same transaction). This is easily established where the subsequent actions are designed to conceal the original act done with *mens rea*. [1992] Q.B. 61

Commentary

(1) The court distinguished *Thabo Meli* (1954) because there was no pre-conceived plan. Moreover, unlike *Thabo Meli* or *Church*, the defendant did not believe he was disposing of a corpse.

(2) The continuous transaction principle dealt with lack of contemporaneity. Even if the second act was the sole cause of the death, liability arose because it was part of the same transaction as the act accompanied by *mens rea*. The court approved a distinction between subsequent acts by which the defendant was trying to assist the victim (such as trying to get the body to hospital) and acts not so designed (such as disposal or trying to conceal the original act). The latter established the continuous transaction whilst the former might not.

(3) The case also raises an issue of causation. If the first act is a contributory cause of the death and accompanied by *mens rea*, there is no difficulty with contemporaneity and the

defendant is guilty because his subsequent acts do not operate as a *novus actus interveniens*. Acts designed to evade liability do not break the chain linking the original act to the death but acts designed to assist the victim might.

---

2. MENS REA

Intention

Key Principle: **Aim, purpose or desire is a type of intention.**

R. v Steane 1947
The defendant was convicted of doing acts likely to assist the enemy with intent to do so, having made war-time broadcasts for the Germans. He appealed on the basis that he acted in order to save his family and not to assist the enemy.

Held: (CA) Appeal allowed. The defendant's actions were consistent with the innocent intention claimed rather than the criminal intent charged because he had acted with the desire of saving his family from a concentration camp. [1947] K.B. 997

Commentary
The court recognised that motive and intention are different concepts but the decision seems not only to equate the two but also to restrict the meaning of intention to desire.

Key Principle: **A result can be intended even though not desired (or wanted).**

R. v Moloney 1985
(see p.16).

Commentary
In explaining the distinction between intention and motive or desire, Lord Bridge gave an example of a man boarding a plane he

knew to be bound for Manchester. Although his aim (motive/desire) was to escape pursuit and he might not actually "want" to go to Manchester, he did, in law, intend to go to there because he knew that he was "morally certain" to arrive there. This recognises that intent has a wider meaning than that given in *Steane*.

Key Principle: **A jury may infer intention from the defendant's foresight of consequences.**

R. v Moloney 1985

A soldier shot and killed his stepfather in response to a drunken challenge. He claimed that he had not aimed the gun at the victim and had, at the time, no idea that firing it would cause injury. The judge directed that intention included both desire and foresight of probable consequences and the defendant was convicted of murder.

Held: (HL) Appeal allowed, manslaughter substituted.

(1) The jury was not directed on the defence that the risk of injury had not crossed the defendant's mind at the time.

(2) The *mens rea* of murder (intention to kill or cause grievous bodily harm) should normally be left to the jury without explanation. However, in rare cases, judges should direct that intention might be inferred if the consequence was foreseen as a natural one by the defendant. Such knowledge or foresight was not equivalent to intention but was, at most, evidence of intention. [1985] A.C. 905

Commentary

(1) The House of Lords confirmed that *Criminal Justice Act 1961*, s.8 abolished the presumption that a person intends the "natural and probable consequences" of their actions. A jury is not bound to infer intention from this alone but must consider all of the evidence.

(2) The case also establishes that intention differs from desire and from foresight of consequences. The latter is simply evidence of intent. Lord Bridge gave five examples of the requisite degree of foresight which referred to levels of high

probability. However, his model direction simply referred to "natural consequences". This caused controversy because of ambiguity in the meaning of "natural consequence". In *R. v Hancock & Shankland* (1986) the House of Lords reaffirmed that foresight of consequences was no more than evidence of intention. However, the House declared the *Moloney* guidelines were unsatisfactory because they omitted reference to probability. In addition to the guidelines, a jury should be directed that the greater the probability of a consequence, the more likely that it was foreseen and therefore also intended. This refines the *Moloney* direction but both cases must now be considered in the light of *R. v Woollin* (below).

Key Principle: **Intention may be established where the defendant foresaw the consequence as a virtually certain result.**

R. v Woollin 1998
The defendant killed his child by throwing him onto a hard surface. Part of the judge's direction suggested that intention could be established if he realised that there was a substantial risk of grievous bodily harm.

Held: (HL) Appeal allowed, manslaughter substituted for murder. Using the phrase "substantial risk" was a misdirection, blurring the distinction between intention and recklessness. The direction from *R. v Nedrick* (1986) (CA) was approved. This direction had been that a jury is not entitled to infer intent unless the defendant appreciated that the consequence was a virtual certainty. [1998] 4 All E.R. 103

Commentary

(1) The case deals only with murder and suggests that intent may not have precisely the same meaning in every context. However it is unlikely that a court would apply a different direction in the case of other crimes of intent.

(2) Whilst confirming the *Nedrick* direction, the House of Lords in this case replaced the word "infer" (used in the *Nedrick* direction) with the word "find". This change in terminology led to the suggestion that the case might have changed the

law as stated in *Moloney* so that foresight of virtual certainty was now a type of intent rather than just evidence of it. However, the case also contains statements that support the view that foresight of virtual certainty remains evidence of intent. This view is confirmed by the Court of Appeal in the subsequent case of *R. v Matthews & Alleyne* (2003).

Recklessness

Key Principle: **Recklessness involves unreasonable risk taking where the defendant is aware of the existence of the risk being taken.**

R. v G and another 2003
Two boys, aged 11 and 12, went camping without their parents' permission. They lit some newspaper in the back yard of a shop and threw it under a large plastic wheelie-bin. They left without putting out the fire. The fire spread to the shop causing over £1,000,000 worth of damage. The boys had expected the lighted newspaper to burn itself out and had not appreciated any risk of the fire spreading in the way it did. They were convicted of arson contrary to s.1 of the *Criminal Damage Act 1971* following a direction based on the definition of recklessness laid down in *R. v Caldwell* (see below). The Court of Appeal dismissed their appeal.

Held: (HL) Defendant's appeal allowed. "A person acts . . . 'recklessly' [within the meaning of s.1 of the 1971 Act] with respect to—

(i) a circumstance when he is aware of a risk that it exists or will exist;

(ii) a result when he is aware of a risk that it will occur;

and it is, in the circumstances known to him, unreasonable to take the risk. . ." [2003] 4 All E.R. 765

Commentary
The definition of recklessness given in this case is based on that given in cl.18(c) of the *Draft Criminal Code (1989)* and confirms the test for recklessness established in *R. v Cunningham* (1957). In that case, the defendant had broken into a gas meter in order to steal the contents. Gas had escaped, partially suffocating the

victim. The defendant's conviction for maliciously administering a noxious thing was quashed by the Court of Appeal because of a misdirection that "maliciously" meant "wickedly". The court held that the word "maliciously" required proof that the defendant either intended injury or was reckless in the sense that he foresaw that injury might be caused but nevertheless went on to take that risk.

This subjective test of advertent recklessness means that those incapable of appreciating risks are not reckless. Thus in *R. v Stephenson* (1979), the defendant's conviction for reckless arson was quashed because he may not have appreciated or considered the risk of damage due to schizophrenia.

Key Principle: **A defendant is not reckless where s/he fails to give thought to the existence of the risk being taken, even though that risk may have been an obvious and serious one.**

R. v G 2003
(see above).

Commentary

(1) In this case the House of Lords decided that only advertent risk taking amounts to recklessness. Inadvertent risk taking is no longer sufficient. In so doing, the House of Lords overruled its earlier decision in the case of *R. v Caldwell* (1982). In *R. v Caldwell*, the defendant set fire to a hotel and claimed to have been so drunk that the risk of endangering lives had not crossed his mind. In deciding that self-induced intoxication was not relevant to the charge under s.1(2) of the *Criminal Damage Act 1971* (see Ch.13), Lord Diplock defined recklessness as including not only recognising a risk and going on to take it but also failing to give any thought to whether there is a risk when, if thought were given, it would be obvious that there was. The House of Lords in *R. v G* concluded that the earlier case had "misconstrued s.1 of the Act" and was "offensive to principle and . . . apt to cause injustice". This was due in part to the fact that the test applied to determine whether a defendant was inadvertently reckless was whether the risk in question would be obvious to a reasonable person. This had led to the conviction of

defendants such as the 14-year-old girl in *Elliott v C (A Minor)* (1983). She had set fire to white spirit which had then destroyed a shed. She had given no thought to the risk and even if she had done so, it was established that the risk would not have been obvious to her. The test applied, with regret, by the Divisional Court was whether the risk would have been obvious to a reasonable person.

(2) The House of Lords rejected the invitation to impose liability for inadvertent reckless where the risk would have been obvious to the defendant if thought had been given. Their Lordships also rejected the possibility of liability arising only where the risk would have been obvious to the reasonable person in the defendant's situation. Liability simply does not now arise for inadvertent risk taking.

(3) Their Lordships made it clear that they were only considering the meaning of reckless in the context of s.1 of the *Criminal Damage Act 1971.* However, even prior to this case, the *Caldwell* test for inadvertent recklessness had been rejected in a number of areas: rape: *R. v Satnam & Kewal* (1983); manslaughter: *R. v Adomako* (1995); crimes of malice: *R. v Savage & Parmenter* (1992). Therefore it seems likely that *R. v G* now provides a definition of recklessness of universal application in criminal law.

Key Principle: **A defendant who considers whether a risk exists and genuinely decides that there is no risk is not reckless.**

Chief Constable of Avon & Somerset v Shimmen 1987

An expert in Korean self-defence was charged with criminal damage having unintentionally broken a window. The court accepted that he was not reckless because, relying on his skill, he had decided that the window would not break.

Held: (DC) Prosecution appeal allowed. Defendants are not reckless if they consider the risk and decide that there is none. However, this defendant had realised that there was some risk but had thought that he could avoid it. Thus he was reckless in the sense of realising a risk and going on to take it. (1987) 84 Cr.App.R. 7, QBD

Commentary
Defendants who consider a risk and decide that there is none do not fall within advertent recklessness because they have not decided to run the risk. This is really no more than an application of the general principle laid down in *DPP v Morgan* (1976) (see p.22) and confirmed in *B (A Child) v DPP* (2000) (see p.23) that a genuine mistake of fact negates *mens rea*.

Transferred Malice

Key Principle: **If the defendant has the *mens rea* of a crime and causes the *actus reus* of that crime against an unforeseen victim, the original *mens rea* is transferred to the actual *actus reus*.**

R. v Latimer 1886
The defendant intended to strike a man but accidentally struck the woman standing next to him. He was convicted under *Offences Against the Person Act 1861*, s.20.

Held: (CCCR) Defendant's appeal dismissed. The defendant was guilty because "if a person has a malicious intent towards one person, and in carrying into effect that malicious intent he injures another . . . he is guilty of what the law considers malice against the person so injured." (1886) 17 Q.B.D. 359

Commentary
The principle applies equally to offences against property. The House of Lords in *Attorney-General's Reference (No.3 of 1994)* (1998) (see p.53) confirmed the existence of the principle although it was deemed to be a fiction without "any sound intellectual basis". On the particular facts of the case, the court refused to apply the principle to murder because it would involve a double transfer of intent (from mother to foetus and from foetus to the child it became). However, it is difficult to see how the proposed conviction for manslaughter was based on anything but such a double transfer.

Key Principle: **Malice can only be transferred if the *actus reus* (for which there is *mens rea*) is the same as the *actus reus* actually committed.**

R. v Pembliton 1874

The defendant aimed a stone at a group of people but it broke a window instead and he was found guilty of criminal damage.

Held: (CCCR) Conviction quashed. Since there was no finding that the defendant was reckless about breaking the window, the intent to strike a person could not provide the *mens rea* for maliciously injuring property. (1872–75) L.R. 2 C.C.R. 119

Commentary

In *Attorney-General's Reference (No.3 of 1994) (1998)* (see p.53), it was said that the principle only applies where the intention is to do a particular kind of harm and that kind of harm is then actually done. This may restrict the principle because it may mean that the *mens rea* of some crimes (for example, intention to cause grievous bodily harm in murder) cannot be transferred to the *actus reus* (killing) unless it is deemed to be the same kind of harm.

Mistake of Fact

Key Principle: **A genuine mistake about the existence of a definitional (*actus reus*) element of a crime negates *mens rea* whether or not that mistake is based on reasonable grounds.**

DPP v Morgan 1976

The defendants were convicted of rape although they claimed a mistaken belief that the woman was consenting. They appealed against the direction that they were only entitled to rely on their belief if it was both honestly and reasonably held.

Held: (HL) Appeal dismissed. There was a misdirection but no miscarriage of justice. The *mens rea* of rape is intention to have intercourse without consent or recklessness, not caring whether there is lack of consent. An honest belief in consent negatives that *mens rea*. The mistake does not also have to be reasonable. [1976] A.C. 182

Commentary

(1) The mistake is not a "defence" but simply denies the prosecution case. Whilst the mistake does not have to be reasonable, lack of reasonable grounds may be evidence that the belief was not genuinely held. This was the reason for applying the proviso on appeal.

(2) The court distinguished *Tolson* (1889) (see p.25) and *Prince* (1875) (see below) as cases dealing with offences that do not require proof of *mens rea*. Cases of defences were also distinguished. Thus, much turns on whether the mistake relates to a "definitional" (*actus reus*) element or a defence element. The same reasoning was used in *Kimber* (1983) (mistake about lack of consent in indecent assault) and in *Williams* (1984) (see Ch.1, p.5) where the word "unlawful" was held to be part of the *actus reus* of assault. Therefore even an unreasonable mistake about the lawfulness of the act negated *mens rea*. This was confirmed in *Beckford* (1988) (see Ch.14, p.167).

(3) Under the *Sexual Offences Act 2003* the law relating to rape has been changed. Rape is now committed unless the defendant reasonably believes that the complainant consents. This would affect the decision in *Morgan* in so far as it deals with rape but it does not affect the general principle laid down in the case.

B (A Child) v Director of Public Prosecutions 2000

The defendant, a 15-year-old boy, was charged with inciting a girl under the age of 14 to commit an act of gross indecency contrary to s.1 of the *Indecency With Children Act 1960*. Although the defendant honestly believed the girl to be over the age of 14, he was convicted on the basis that the age element in the offence was one of strict liability.

Held: (HL) Defendant's appeal allowed. Section 1(1) of the *Indecency With Children Act 1960* did not create a strict liability offence. A defendant was entitled to an acquittal if he held the honest belief that the child was aged 14 or over. The belief did not have to be based on reasonable grounds. [2000] 2 A.C. 428

Commentary

(1) The House of Lords in *R. v K* (2001) reached a similar decision in relation to a charge of indecently assaulting a girl under the age of 16. Note that the law in both of these areas has been changed by the *Sexual Offences Act 2003*. However this does not affect the general principle represented by the above case law.

(2) The case confirms that the *Morgan* principle is one of general application to offences that require proof of *mens rea* and that it represents a common law principle that is to

be preferred to that laid down in *R. v Tolson* (see p.25). The case also confirms that the burden of proof is on the prosecution to establish lack of honest belief.

Key Principle: **A mistake about the existence of a definitional (*actus reus*) element of a crime is irrelevant (even where genuine and reasonable) if the element is one of strict liability and not afforded a defence of mistake.**

R. v Prince 1875

The defendant was convicted of abducting a girl under the age of 16. He appealed on the basis that he reasonably believed that she was aged 18.

Held: (CCCR) Appeal dismissed. The statute did not specify *mens rea* in respect of the age. That element was therefore one of strict liability and since the girl was, in fact, under the age of 16 the defendant was guilty. [1874–80] All E.R. 881

Commentary

(1) The court distinguished other elements of the offence for which *mens rea* was required and where mistake might excuse the defendant.

(2) Not only did the statute not provide for *mens rea* in respect of "age" but it also provided no defence. Contrast *Tolson* (see below).

(3) Prior to the passing of the *Sexual Offences Act 2003*, the decision in *B (A Child) v DPP* (2000) (see above and Ch.3, p.26) had thrown doubt on the decision in *R. v Prince* in so far as it dealt with abduction. However, this did not affect the general principle and mistakes about strict liability elements are still irrelevant.

Key Principle: **In some cases, a mistake about the existence of a definitional (*actus reus*) element of a crime, which need not be accompanied by *mens rea*, may excuse if based on reasonable grounds.**

R. v Tolson 1889
The defendant was convicted of bigamy. She remarried whilst her first husband was alive, genuinely and reasonably believing that he was dead.

Held: (CCCR) Defendant's appeal allowed. The relevant statute did not require proof of *mens rea* in respect of "being married". However, it did not exclude (either expressly or implicitly) a defence of honest and reasonable belief that the first husband was dead. The defendant, who honestly and reasonably believed that she was no longer married, was not guilty of bigamy. (1889) L.R. 23 Q.B.D. 168

Commentary
The court distinguished *Prince* (1875) where the policy behind the offence was such that there was no defence of reasonable mistake. It had been suggested that *Tolson* created a general (objective) principle that mistaken belief had to be both honest and reasonable to exonerate a defendant. This is rejected in *B (A Child) v DPP* (2000) (see p.23 and Ch.3, p.26). The principle of general application is now that of (subjective) honest belief. This may mean that the decision in relation to bigamy in *Tolson* is incorrect. Alternatively it may be that bigamy is an exception to the general principle being, in effect, an example of a crime of negligence rather than *mens rea*. A mistake about an element satisfied by negligence would still need to be based on reasonable grounds.

Key Principle: **Where a mistake relates to an issue of defence rather than to the existence of a definitional element, the requirements for successfully pleading mistake vary according to the type of defence in question.**

Albert v Lavin 1981
The defendant hit an off-duty policeman in plain clothes, who was trying to restrain him to prevent a breach of the peace. The defendant mistakenly believed that he was being unlawfully attacked and so was entitled to defend himself. The question was whether he had assaulted the policeman which depended on whether he could rely on his belief that he was acting lawfully or whether he could only do so if it was based on reasonable grounds. This turned on whether the element of

"unlawfulness" was a matter of defence or part of the definition of the offence.

Held: (DC) "Unlawfulness" was a defence issue and not part of the *actus reus* of assault. Relying on *Morgan,* mistakes affecting *mens rea* are tested subjectively but mistakes relating to defences are tested objectively. Therefore the defendant was guilty of assault because his belief (as to self-defence) had to be both genuine and reasonable. [1981] 2 W.L.R. 1070

Commentary
It is now clear that the analysis adopted (that "unlawful" was a defence element) is incorrect (see *Williams* and *Beckford*). Therefore, where they affect the *mens rea* of a crime, mistakes about self-defence now fall within the key principle illustrated by *Morgan.* It is also clear that it is no longer generally correct to say that mistakes about defences are tested objectively. See Chs 6 and 14.

---

3. STRICT LIABILITY

Key Principle: **Where a statute does not refer to a state of mind, there is a presumption in favour of *mens rea.***

B (A Child) v Director of Public Prosecutions 2000
(see p.23).

Held: (HL) Defendant's appeal allowed. Section 1(1) of the *Indecency With Children Act 1960* did not create a strict liability offence and the prosecution was required to prove *mens rea.* Where a statute makes no reference to *mens rea* "the starting point for a court is the established common law presumption that a mental element, traditionally labelled *mens rea,* is an essential ingredient. . ." *per* Lord Nicholls. [2000] 2 A.C. 428

Commentary
Lord Steyn refers to the presumption as an element of the "principle of legality" under which Parliament is assumed to have legislated. Judgments in the cases of *Sweet v Parsley* (1970) (see

p.31) and *Gammon v Attorney-General of Hong Kong* (1985) (see p.31) were cited with approval. In the former, Lord Reid said ". . . whenever a section is silent as to *mens rea*, there is a presumption that . . . we must read in words appropriate to require *mens rea*". In the latter, the Privy Council listed a number of factors to be considered in determining whether an offence was one of strict liability. The first was that "there is a presumption of law that *mens rea* is required".

Key Principle: **The presumption in favour of *mens rea* can only be displaced by necessary implication.**

B (A Child) v Director of Public Prosecutions 2000
(see above).

Commentary
Their Lordships made clear that if Parliament had not expressly excluded *mens rea*, strict liability should not be imposed just because it was reasonable to infer that it was intended. The need for *mens rea* could only be negatived by necessary implication which "connotes an implication which is compellingly clear". Factors that might be taken into account in deciding whether there was such an implication included "the language used, the nature of the offence, the mischief sought to be prevented and any other circumstances which may assist. . ." *per* Lord Nicholls.

Key Principle: **In determining whether strict liability is a necessary implication, the court will consider the statutory words used in describing the offence.**

Alphacell v Woodward 1972
Pumps failed to work properly which caused polluted water to overflow from the defendant's tanks. The company was convicted of "causing" pollution and appealed on the basis that the offence required proof of *mens rea*.

Held: (HL) Appeal dismissed. The word "cause" was not accompanied by *mens rea* words and did not in itself imply *mens rea*. It was a strict liability offence. [1972] A.C. 824

Commentary
Other statutory words have also been held to create strict liability. For example, "using" (as in using a vehicle in contravention of regulations: *James & Son v Smee* (1955)) and "possession" (see *Warner v Metropolitan Police Commissioner* (1969) below). Other words import *mens rea*, such as "permitting", "allowing", and "suffering". Even "causing" in a different context from that in *Alphacell* has been held to import *mens rea*: *James & Son v Smee* (1955) (causing another to contravene the regulations). The next case is another illustration of a word interpreted as importing *mens rea*.

Sweet v Parsley 1970
A landlady was charged with being concerned in the management of premises, used for the purpose of smoking cannabis. She occasionally visited the premises but was unaware of the cannabis smoking. She was convicted on the basis of strict liability.

Held: (HL) Defendant's appeal allowed. The offence was not one of strict liability. Considering the words of the statute in question, the House decided that it must be the manager's purpose (intention) that the premises be used for the smoking of cannabis or, at the very minimum, it must be shown that she knew of the purpose to which the premises were put. [1970] A.C. 132

Commentary
The decision was confirmed by *Misuse of Drugs Act 1971*, s.8 which specifically requires proof of knowledge.

Warner v Metropolitan Police Commissioner 1969
The defendant was convicted of possessing amphetamine sulphate, found in a box in his possession which he claimed to believe contained scent.

Held: (HL) Defendant's appeal dismissed. "Possession" of drugs is a strict liability offence. It requires proof that the defendant knew he had control over something (which was in fact a drug) but not that he knew that it was a drug. Where the drug is in a container, possession of the container gives rise to an inference of possession of the contents. The defendant may displace this inference by proving that he was mistaken as to the nature (not merely quality) of the contents and, that as a servant or bailee, he had no right to open the container and had no reason to suspect that it contained drugs; or, that as an owner, he received the package innocently and had no reasonable opportunity to ascertain the nature of the contents. [1969] 2 A.C. 256

Commentary
The court stressed that the meaning of "possession" might differ in other contexts. Whilst possessing a drug is strict liability, the case also provides a defence of lack of negligence in "container cases". The offence was re-enacted in the *Misuse of Drugs Act 1971* which specifically provides a no-negligence defence.

Key Principle: **In determining whether strict liability is a necessary implication, the court may consider whether *mens rea* words (or defences) appear elsewhere in the statute.**

Cundy v Le Cocq 1884
A licensee was charged with selling alcohol to an intoxicated person when neither he nor his servants realised that the purchaser was intoxicated. He was convicted on the basis of strict liability and appealed.

Held: (DC) Appeal dismissed. Other sections of the *Licensing Act 1872* use the word "knowingly" whilst s.13, the section under consideration, did not. This was strong evidence that the offence was intended to be one of strict liability. [1884] L.R. 13 Q.B.D. 207

Commentary
Compare the next case.

Sherras v De Rutzen 1895
The defendant licensee served alcohol to a police constable, believing that he was off-duty.

Held: (DC) Conviction quashed because the offence (contrary to s.16(2) of the *Licensing Act 1872*) required proof of *mens rea*. Moreover, generally "there is a presumption that *mens rea*, an evil intention, or knowledge of the wrongfulness of the act, is an essential ingredient in every offence. . ." *per* Wright J. [1895] 1 Q.B. 918

Commentary

The court accepted that the presumption of *mens rea* may "be displaced . . . by the words of the statute creating the offence . . ." but was not prepared to infer strict liability simply because the section did not use the word "knowingly" whilst other sections did.

Pharmaceutical Society v Storkwain 1986

The defendants were charged under *Medicines Act 1968*, s.58(2)(a) with supplying medicine on forged prescriptions. They believed that the prescriptions were valid and were originally acquitted but the Divisional Court held that the offence was strict.

Held: (HL) Defendant's appeal dismissed. Various sections in the Act expressly provided for *mens rea* and so it could be inferred that the omission to do so in s.58(2)(a) was deliberate. Thus the offence was strict. [1986] 1 W.L.R. 903

Commentary

Compare *Pharmaceutical Society v Harwood* (1981) where a prosecution under *Medicines Act 1968*, s.58(2)(a) for supplying medicine on an incorrect prescription failed because the court decided that the section required proof of *mens rea*.

Key Principle: **The court may also consider the wording of similar offences in other statutes.**

B (A Child) v Director of Public Prosecutions 2000

(see p.23). The prosecution argued that s.1(1) of the *Indecency with Children Act 1960* should be read in the light of the *Sexual Offences Act 1956*. Several sections of the 1956 Act, clearly or by implication, create strict liability in respect of sexual offences involving persons under 16.

Held: (HL) Defendant's appeal allowed. The 1956 Act was a consolidating statute and was "not the product of a rational scheme" *per* Lord Steyn. It did not display a "clear and coherent pattern" *per* Lord Nicholls and therefore could not be relied upon to establish strict liability under s.1(1) of the *Indecency With Children Act 1960*. [2000] 2 A.C. 428

Commentary
Lord Nicholls stated that, generally, the interpretation to be given to a statute could only be gleaned from another statute where that gave "compelling guidance" and consistency of theme. See also the decision in *R. v K* (2001) where provisions of ss.14 and 15 of the *Sexual Offences Act 1956* (now repealed) other than the one under consideration were not conclusive as an aid to interpretation because they were not part of a "single, coherent legislative scheme" *per* Lord Bingham.

Key Principle: **If the words are not conclusive, the presumption of *mens rea* may be displaced by extrinsic factors such as the subject matter of the offence (including the stigma which it may attract).**

Sweet v Parsley 1970
(see p.28).

Held: (HL) In considering whether an offence is strict, Lord Reid added to *Sherras* that the subject matter of the offence must be taken into account. According to Wright J. in *Sherras,* the offence was one which was "not criminal in any real sense, but . . . which (is prohibited) . . . in the public interest". According to Lord Reid such "quasi-crimes" are less likely to require *mens rea* than "truly criminal" acts. When considering the latter, regard must also be given to factors such as the stigma that attaches to the offence, its gravity and whether public interest is served by strict liability. [1970] A.C. 132

Commentary
In *B (A Child)* (2000), above, Lord Steyn approved the distinction between true and quasi crimes. Section 1(1) of the *Indecency with Children Act 1960* fell within the former category. The seriousness of the offence, the social stigma attached and the broad terms in which it was drawn all militated against strict liability.

Gammon Ltd v Attorney-General of Hong Kong 1985
The defendants were convicted of offences under a Building Ordinance for deviating from plans and carrying out works in a way likely to risk injury or damage.

Held: (PC) Defendant's appeal dismissed. The conditions are to be considered in determining whether an offence is strict are:

(1) the presumption of *mens rea;*

(2) the presumption is strongest where the offence is "truly criminal" in nature;

(3) "the presumption . . . can be displaced only if this is clearly or by necessary implication the effect of the statute";

(4) "the only situation in which the presumption can be displaced is where the statute is concerned with an issue of social concern, and public safety is such an issue. . .".

Since the overall purpose of the Ordinance was the protection of public safety, the offences were ones of strict liability. [1985] 1 A.C. 1

Commentary

(1) In the next case, *Lim Chin Aik* (1963), Lord Evershed also referred to the relevance of the subject matter in deciding on strict liability. He said that such liability was frequently inferred where the subject was the regulation of public welfare.

(2) Other examples where the court has referred to social concern or grave social evil as a reason for imposing strict liability include the supply of medicines: *Storkwain* (1986), pollution: *Alphacell* (1972) and the possession of drugs: *Warner* (1969). In *R. v Prince* (1875) a similar argument was used in the case of abduction. Prior to *B (A Child)* (2000) it had been assumed that *Prince* created a general principle of strict liability in relation to age-based sexual offences. However, this was rejected in *B (A Child)* despite recognition that sexual exploitation of the young was a great social evil. The case confirms that grave social evil is not the only consideration. This point was also made by Lord Evershed in *Lim Chin Aik* (1963).

Key Principle: **Generally, strict liability should not be imposed unless it will promote greater vigilance and assist in preventing the offence.**

Lim Chin Aik v R. 1963

The defendant was convicted of contravening a statutory provision regarding entry to Singapore. An order prohibiting his entry was issued but there was no evidence that he was aware of this.

Held: (PC) Defendant's appeal allowed. The offence required proof of *mens rea.* In addition to considering the social evil, regard must be given to whether strict liability would "assist in the enforcement of the regulations. . . . Where . . . strict liability would result in . . . conviction of a class of persons whose conduct could not in any way affect the observance of the law . . . even where the statute is dealing with a grave social evil, strict liability is not likely to be intended." [1963] A.C. 160

Gammon Ltd v Attorney-General of Hong Kong 1985
(see p.31).

Held: (PC) "The presumption of *mens rea* stands unless it can be shown that the creation of strict liability will be effective to promote the objects of the statute by encouraging greater vigilance to prevent the commission of the offence." Their Lordships concluded that imposing strict liability would help to do so in this case. [1985] 1 A.C. 1

Commentary
In *Storkwain* (1986) (see p.30), Lord Goff rejected the argument that strict liability should not be imposed because it would not "tend towards greater efficiency on the part of pharmacists in detecting forged prescriptions". However, in *Sweet v Parsley* (1970) (see p.28), Lord Reid was influenced by the fact that even "The greatest vigilance cannot prevent tenants . . . from smoking cannabis . . . in their own rooms" and Lord Diplock stated that "strict liability should not easily be inferred, particularly if there is nothing the defendant could do to improve, influence or control the situation". Moreover, another factor taken into account in rejecting strict liability in *B (A Child)* (2000) was the fact that, according to Lord Nicholls, "there is no general agreement that strict liability is necessary to the enforcement of the law protecting children in sexual matters". Compare this view with that of the legislature as evidenced in the *Sexual Offences Act 2003*.

4. NON-FATAL OFFENCES AGAINST THE PERSON

Common Assault and Battery

Key Principle: **The *actus reus* of assault involves an act causing apprehension of unlawful personal violence.**

Fagan v Metropolitan Police Commissioner 1969
(see Ch.1, p.1).

Held: (DC) Deciding that assault cannot be committed by omission, the court defined assault as "an act which . . . causes another person to apprehend immediate and unlawful personal violence". [1969] 1 Q.B. 439

Commentary
Apprehension of violence is satisfied by proof of anticipation of a battery. The *actus reus* includes that the force apprehended be unlawful, according to *Williams* (1984) (confirmed in *Beckford*).

Key Principle: **The victim must apprehend immediate force or violence.**

R. v Ireland & Burstow 1998
Ireland was convicted of assault occasioning actual bodily harm, having made repeated silent telephone calls to the victims, causing them psychological damage.

Held: (HL) Appeal dismissed. Silent telephone calls were capable of amounting to assault if the victim apprehended immediate unlawful violence. [1998] A.C. 147

Commentary
This allows for a liberal interpretation of immediacy. Whether or not there is an assault depends on all the circumstances including what it was that the victim apprehended. The case also confirms

that assault can be committed by words alone. A similar position on both points had been taken in *R. v Constanza* (1997) (CA).

Key Principle: **The *actus reus* of battery involves using unlawful force without the victim's consent.**

Fagan v Metropolitan Police Commissioner 1969
(see Ch.1, p.1).

Held: (DC) Deciding that battery cannot be committed by omission, the court defined battery as the "use of unlawful force to another person without his consent". [1969] 1 Q.B. 439

Commentary
The term "force" is satisfied simply by proof of contact (or "touching", see *Faulkner v Talbot* (1981)) and the force must be unlawful (see *Williams* (1984)). It has also been suggested, *obiter*, in *Haystead v Chief Constable of Derbyshire* (2000) that it is probably not necessary to show that the force was directly inflicted.

Key Principle: **Consent to contact generally prevents liability.**

Attorney-General's Reference (No.6 of 1980)
Two young men agreed to settle an argument by fighting and one sustained a bleeding nose and bruises. The other was acquitted of assault on a direction that the agreement to fight (and the use of reasonable force) prevented liability.

Held: (QBD) Consent was no defence for reasons given below but "ordinarily if the victim consents, the assailant is not guilty". [1981] 2 All E.R. 1057

Commentary
It was also confirmed in *R. v Brown* (1994) (see p.38) that consent may be a defence to assault.

Key Principle: **Consent to contact does not necessarily include consent to the consequences of the contact.**

R. v Dica 2004

The defendant was HIV positive and had unprotected consensual sexual intercourse with two women in the course of long term relationships with them. Both became infected as a result. It was not alleged that the defendant had intended to infect the women. The defendant was convicted of recklessly inflicting grievous bodily harm, contrary to s.20 of the *Offences Against the Person Act 1861*.

Held: (CA) Appeal allowed, retrial ordered for reasons explained below. Consent to the act of sexual intercourse is not to be regarded "as consent to the risk of consequent disease". [2004] 3 All E.R. 593

Commentary

This departs from the decision in *R. v Clarence* (1889) (below) where the defendant was held not to have assaulted his wife because she had consented to the act (of sexual intercourse) which had caused the infection with venereal disease. According to *Dica* there are two issues for consideration in these cases: consent to the sexual intercourse and consent to the injury or infection. Establishing consent to the act is not enough to secure an acquittal.

Key Principle: **Fraud or mistake vitiate apparent consent in certain circumstances.**

R. v Clarence 1889

The defendant was convicted of inflicting grievous bodily harm and assault occasioning actual bodily harm on his wife, having infected her with gonorrhoea during consensual intercourse. He appealed on the basis of consent and the prosecution argued that the wife would not have consented if she had known of her husband's condition.

Held: (CCCR) Appeal allowed. Fraud only vitiates consent if it relates to the nature of the act or identity of the actor. Consent was not obtained by fraud as to either of these factors and so there was no assault. (1888) 22 Q.B.D. 23

Commentary

(1) Although this decision is disapproved of in *R. v Dica* (2004) the Court of Appeal did not directly refer to this aspect of the case.

(2) Following *Clarence*, identity of the actor does not extend to the attributes of the person. This point was also made in *R. v Richardson* (1998) (CA) where consent to dental treatment was not vitiated by the fact that the defendant had been disqualified from practice. However, that decision should be contrasted with the following case which suggests that the qualifications of the defendant may be relevant to the nature and quality of the act.

Key Principle: **A mistake as to the nature or quality of the act may, in some circumstances, vitiate consent.**

R v Tabassum 2000

The defendant obtained consent for a breast examination from three women. He had indicated that he was involved in a breast cancer survey and the women consented in the mistaken belief that he had relevant medical qualifications or training. The defendant appealed against conviction for indecent assault.

Held: (CA) Appeal dismissed. The women consented to what they believed was a medical examination by a person with medical qualifications. Although they had consented to the nature of the act (a breast examination) their consent was vitiated because they had not consented to its quality. [2000] 2 Cr.App.R. 328

Commentary

This is the first case to suggest that mistakes as to the quality of the act (rather than as to its nature) may vitiate consent and it should be compared with *R. v Clarence* (above). It was Tabassum's lack of medical qualifications that affected the quality of the act. This should be compared with *R. v Richardson* (1998) which was argued as a case of mistaken identity rather than as one of mistake as to nature or quality of the act. It may be possible to distinguish

Tabassum as a case where the lack of qualifications affected the purpose of the act.

Key Principle: **Subject to public policy exceptions, consent is no defence where actual bodily harm is caused and was a likely or an intended consequence of the assault.**

R. v Donovan 1934
The defendant caused bruising in the course of consensually caning a woman for sexual gratification. He appealed against conviction for indecent and common assault.

Held: (CCA) Appeal allowed. Nevertheless, the court indicated that, generally, consent was no defence where actual bodily harm was intended or a probable consequence of the activity. Public policy exceptions to the rule included "mutual manly contests" and "rough and undisciplined sport or play, where there is no anger and no intention to cause bodily harm". [1934] 2 K.B. 498

Commentary
For the meaning of actual bodily harm, see below. An example of one of the exceptions noted in *Donovan* is illustrated in *Jones* (1986) where "rough and undisciplined play", causing grievous bodily harm, gave rise to no liability because the defendants did not intend to cause harm and believed that the victim consented. In *Attorney-General's Reference (No.6 of 1980)* (1981), the court held that consent was no defence where actual bodily harm was intended and/or caused because "it is not in the public interest that people should try to cause or should cause each other actual bodily harm for no good reason". It made no difference whether the fight occurred in public or private. The public interest exceptions included properly conducted games and sports, lawful chastisement, reasonable surgical interference and dangerous exhibitions.

R. v Brown 1994
The defendants caused actual bodily harm and wounding in the course of consensual sado-masochistic activities. They were convicted and appealed.

Held: (HL) Appeals dismissed. Public policy and public interest did not require that the defence of consent be extended to inflicting bodily harm in the course of sado-masochistic practices. [1994] 1 A.C. 212

Commentary
The policy exceptions mentioned in *Donovan* and *Attorney-General's Reference* (1981) were noted (and ritual circumcision and tattooing were added). The majority rejected the defence argument that the activities in *Brown* were of a sexual nature (in which case consent might have been a defence). In the court's view, sado-masochism was "violent", "cruel" and "degrading" behaviour and so there was no public interest in allowing consent as a defence. This can be contrasted with the decision in *R. v Wilson* (1997). In *Wilson*, the Court of Appeal held that consent was a defence to inflicting actual bodily harm when the defendant burned his initials into his wife's buttocks (at her instigation). The activity lacked the extreme and aggressive element present in *Brown* and was akin to tattooing. Public policy and interest did not demand that such an activity, carried out consensually between spouses in private, should amount to an offence. *Wilson* was distinguished in *R. v Emmett* (1999) where the defendant caused harm to his female sexual partner in the course of consensual sado-masochistic practices. The activities included semi-asphyxiation and the infliction of third-degree burns. *R. v Brown* (1994) was applied because of the nature of the activities and injuries: one was life-threatening and the other involved very serious injury.

Key Principle: **Subject to public policy exceptions, consent is no defence to the intentional infliction of grievous bodily harm on another.**

R. v Dica (2004)
(above).

Commentary
The court commented *obiter* that consent would be no defence where a defendant deliberately infected or spread HIV with intent to cause grievous bodily harm. This was considered to be an application of the principle in *R. v Brown* (1994).

Key Principle: **Consent to running the risk of injury may be a defence to unintentional but reckless infliction of grievous bodily harm.**

R. v Dica (2004)
(above).

Held: Consent to the risk of disease transmitted through sexual intercourse might be a defence if a defendant had been no more than reckless as to the risk of the transmission.

Commentary
These were the issues about which a retrial was ordered in the case. It is also possible, following *R. v Slingsby (Simon)* (1995), that consent to just the act operates as a defence where neither the defendant nor the victim are reckless as to the risk of serious injury. In *Slingsby*, the defendant was acquitted of manslaughter having caused the death of his sexual partner by consensually engaging in an activity which neither of them realised would cause serious injury.

Key Principle: **The *mens rea* of assault and battery is satisfied by either intention or recklessness.**

R. v Venna 1976
The defendant was convicted of assault occasioning actual bodily harm, having fractured a bone in a policeman's hand whilst being arrested. He appealed against a direction that recklessness was sufficient *mens rea* for battery.

Held: (CA) Appeal dismissed. The *mens rea* of battery "is satisfied by proof that the defendant intentionally or recklessly applied force to the person of another". [1976] Q.B. 421

Commentary
The same *mens rea* satisfies assault (intentionally or recklessly causing another person to apprehend violence). Moreover, according to *Williams* (see Ch.1), the *mens rea* extends to the element of "unlawfulness" so that a belief that force is lawful denies the

prosecution case. The *mens rea* similarly extends to "lack of consent". *Offences Against the Person Act 1861*, s.47.

Key Principle: ***Offences Against the Person Act 1861,*** **s.47 requires proof of common assault or battery.**

R. v Venna 1976
(see above).

Commentary
Both this and *Williams* are cases of assault occasioning actual bodily harm under s.47 where liability turned on proving a common assault (or battery). The common assault/battery must cause the actual bodily harm in fact and law. For the rules on causation, see Ch.1 and, for example, *R. v Roberts* (1972) (see p.42).

Key Principle: **"Actual bodily harm" is temporary or permanent bodily injury, not so "trivial as to be wholly insignificant".**

R. v Donovan 1934
(see p.38).

Held: (CCA) "Bodily harm has its ordinary meaning and includes any hurt or injury calculated to interfere with the health or comfort of the prosecutor . . . it need not be permanent but must . . . be more than merely transient and trifling". [1934] 2 K.B. 498

Commentary
In *R. (on the application of T) v DPP* (2003) this was interpreted to include a momentary loss of consciousness which though "transitory" was not "trifling".

Key Principle: **Actual bodily harm includes psychiatric injury.**

R. v Ireland & Burstow 1998
(see pp.34 and 44).

Held: (HL) Recognisable psychiatric illness is capable of amounting to bodily harm. [1998] A.C. 147

Commentary
The case approves the decision in *R. v Chan-Fook* (1994) that actual bodily harm embraces psychiatric injury which goes beyond mere "fear, distress or panic".

Key Principle: **The *mens rea* of s.47 is the same as for common assault and does not require proof of *mens rea* in relation to the actual bodily harm.**

R. v Roberts 1972
The defendant was convicted of s.47, after assaulting a woman in his car by trying to remove her coat. She jumped from the car, sustaining actual bodily harm. The defendant's appeal included the claim that it was necessary to prove that he foresaw that she might jump from the car.

Held: (CA) Appeal dismissed. The prosecution must prove that the defendant caused the injury in fact and law. This was established since the woman's response was reasonably foreseeable as likely to happen as a result of the defendant's conduct. It was not necessary to show that he foresaw that this might happen. (1971) 56 Cr.App.R. 95

Commentary

(1) The chain of causation is broken if the victim does something "so daft" that the reasonable person would not foresee it (see Ch.1).

(2) Roberts was approved in *Savage & Parmenter* (1992) where the House of Lords confirmed that the prosecution only have to prove the *mens rea* of assault and not intention or recklessness *vis-a-vis* the actual bodily harm.

Offences Against the Person Act 1861, s.20

Key Principle: **The *actus reus* of s.20 requires proof of either wounding or an infliction of grievous bodily harm. A wound requires proof that the whole continuity of the skin is broken.**

C. v Eisenhower 1984
The defendant shot the victim with an air pistol causing bruising and rupturing internal blood vessels in his eye. The defendant appealed against conviction for s.20 on the basis that there was no wound.

Held: (DC) Appeal allowed. Breaking the skin of an internal cavity is sufficient where that skin is continuous with the outer skin of the body. A ruptured blood vessel in itself was insufficient evidence of a break in the continuity of the whole skin. [1984] 1 Q.B. 331

Commentary
The epidermis and dermis must be broken for there to be a wound.

Key Principle: **Grievous bodily harm means "serious bodily harm".**

DPP v Smith 1961
The defendant caused the death of a policeman, who was hanging onto his car, by driving the car into oncoming traffic.

Held: (HL) In dealing with murder, the House commented that grievous bodily harm bears "its ordinary and natural meaning". The meaning of "bodily harm" was self-evident and grievous meant "really serious". [1961] A.C. 290

Commentary
Grievous bodily harm includes serious psychiatric injury (*R. v Ireland & Burstow* (1998) (see below)).

Key Principle: **"Inflicting" can occur without physical violence being applied directly or indirectly to the victim.**

R. v Ireland & Burstow 1998

Burstow, a "stalker", had harassed the victim in a number of ways causing her severe depression. He appealed against conviction on the basis that he could not be said to have inflicted grievous bodily harm because he had not come into contact with the victim.

Held: (HL) Appeal dismissed. Direct or indirect application of force was not a necessary element of the offence. [1998] A.C. 147

Commentary

The House of Lords rejected the argument that assault or battery were elements of the offence. This was applied in *R. v Dica* (2004) which expressly overrules *R. v Clarence* (1888) on this point.

Key Principle: **The *mens rea* of s.20 requires proof that the defendant intended or foresaw the risk of some physical harm.**

R. v Savage & Parmenter 1992

Savage intended to throw the contents of a glass at the victim but let go of the glass, causing a wound. She was convicted under s.20 but because of a misdirection on the *mens rea* of s.20 of the offence, the Court of Appeal substituted a verdict of s.47. Parmenter was convicted of causing grievous bodily harm to his baby. Because of a misdirection on the *mens rea,* the Court of Appeal considered a verdict of s.47 but concluded that the *mens rea* had not been established and so quashed the conviction. Both cases raised the same issues on appeal.

Held: (HL): Dismissing the appeal of Savage and allowing the appeal of Parmenter but substituting a conviction under s.47.

(1) Both defendants could be found guilty under s.47, having been charged with s.20 (see above).

(2) Section 47 could be established even though the defendant did not intend actual bodily harm nor was reckless as to causing it. Therefore both defendants could be convicted under s.47 (and the Court of Appeal had reached the wrong conclusion in the case of *Parmenter*).

(3) It was not necessary, under s.20, to prove that the defendant intended or foresaw a wound or serious physical injury. Intention or recklessness as to some physical harm, albeit minor, was sufficient. [1992] 1 A.C. 699

Commentary

These cases also establish that a verdict of s.47 can be returned on a charge of s.20.

Offences Against the Person Act 1861, s.18

Key Principle: **Section 18, like s.20, requires proof of a wound or grievous bodily harm but, unlike s.20, refers to causing rather than inflicting grievous bodily harm. The word "cause" is wider than the word "inflict".**

R. v Mandair 1995

The defendant caused serious injury to his wife. He was charged under s.18 with causing grievous bodily harm with intent and found guilty of causing grievous bodily harm contrary to s.20 on a direction that this was an alternative, lesser verdict open to the jury.

Held: (HL) "Causing grievous bodily harm" (s.18) could occur by inflicting the harm or by causing it in some other way. Since the word "cause" was wide enough to cover "infliction", a verdict under s.20 was possible on a charge under s.18. Although the verdict of "causing grievous bodily harm contrary to s.20" was inappropriate because the offence under s.20 is one of "inflicting grievous bodily harm", there had been no miscarriage of justice. [1995] 1 A.C. 208

Commentary

(1) Whilst this case suggests a difference between "causing" and "inflicting" grievous bodily harm, in *Ireland & Burstow*, Lord Hope suggested that, for all practical purposes, there is no difference between "cause" and "inflict" beyond the latter implying something detrimental to the victim.

(2) Section 18 requires proof of an ulterior intention to cause grievous bodily harm or to resist or prevent arrest. Foresight of virtual certainty is evidence of this ulterior intent: *R. v Bryson* (1985). It is as yet undecided whether *R. v Woollin* (1998) (see Ch.2) applies to intent under this section.

5. SEXUAL OFFENCES

Rape: The Actus Reus

Key Principle: **The *actus reus* of rape requires proof of non-consensual penile penetration of vagina, anus or mouth. (*Sexual Offences Act 2003*, s.1(1)).**

Commentary

(1) The *actus reus* of rape was originally restricted to vaginal penetration. This definition was extended by the *Criminal Justice and Public Order Act 1994* to include anal penetration. Section 1(1) of the *Sexual Offences Act 2003* represents a further extension of the definition and includes oral penetration.

(2) The term "sexual intercourse" has been replaced by the term "penetration" but the crime is still gender specific in that it requires that the penetration be by penis. However this, like all references to body parts in the Act, now specifically includes those that have been surgically reconstructed: s.79(3). Section 79(2) of the Act preserves the effect of *Kaitamaki v R.* (1985) by providing that "penetration is a continuing act from entry to withdrawal".

(3) In all cases where the complainant is aged 13 or above the prosecution must establish that the penetration was non-consensual in order to prove rape. The meaning of consent is explored in the next key principles. Where the complainant is aged under 13, rape occurs irrespective of consent: s.5 of the *Sexual Offences Act 2003*. Where the complainant is aged between 13 and 16 (or 18 in the case of abuse of trust) there is an alternative charge to rape for cases of consensual penetration. This is the offence of sexual activity with a child contrary to s.9 (and s.16 in the case of abuse of trust).

Key Principle: **A person does not consent to penetration if the defendant intentionally deceived that person as to the nature or purpose of the act. (*Sexual Offences Act 2003*, s.76(2)(a)).**

Commentary

(1) This preserves the decision in cases such as *R. v Flattery* (1877) where the defendant was convicted of rape having intentionally deceived the complainant into believing that the act of sexual intercourse was a surgical operation. For a further example, see the case of *R. v Williams* (1923).

(2) It is less clear what the effect of the Act might be on other previous decisions because it is not yet clear how the court will interpret the meaning of the words "nature" and "purpose" in the Act. It is possible that the word "nature" might be interpreted narrowly in line with the decision in the now otherwise discredited authority of *R. v Clarence* (1889) (see Ch.4, p.36). An alternative approach might be that adopted in *R. v Tabassum* (2000) (see Ch.4 p.37) although this suggests that a mistake as to the quality of the act (rather than its nature) might also vitiate consent. Deliberate deception as to the purpose of the act (s.76(2)(a)) appears to be a new addition to the pre-existing state of the law and would cover where a defendant deliberately deceives the complainant about why the act is being done.

Key Principle: **A person does not consent to penetration if the defendant intentionally induced the consent by impersonating a person known personally to the complainant. (*Sexual Offences Act 2003*, s.76(2)(b)).**

Commentary

This provision confirms and possibly extends the law beyond the decision in *R. v Elbekkay* (1995) where a woman had consented to penetration in the belief that the defendant was her co-habitee. The defendant appealed against conviction on the basis that whilst rape included intercourse obtained by impersonation of a husband (*Sexual Offences Act 1956*, s.1(2)), the same did not apply to other cases of impersonation. The Court of Appeal dismissed the appeal and held that the question was simply whether the woman consented (*Olugboja* (1982)) and she had not consented to intercourse with the defendant in this case.

Key Principle: **In all other cases, a person consents to**

penetration if s/he agrees by choice and has the freedom and capacity to make that choice. (*Sexual Offences Act 2003*, s.74).

Commentary

(1) This provides statutory guidance where previously the matter was left to the decision of the jury: see *R. v Olugboja* (1982).

(2) If the facts of a case like *R. v Clarence* fell outside the law as laid down in s.76(2)(a) they would still be caught by this section. Likewise with the facts of *R. v Linekar* (1995) so that the question in that case would be whether the deceit about payment prevented the woman from agreeing to the penetration by choice with freedom and capacity to make that choice.

Key Principle: **There is a presumption that consent is lacking in certain situations.The presumption may be rebutted by evidence from the defendant. (*Sexual Offences Act 2003*, s.75(1)).**

Key Principle: **The circumstances in which there is a rebuttable presumption of lack of consent are:**

Section 75(2)(a): Where "any person was, at the time of the relevant act or immediately before it began, using violence against the complainant or causing the complainant to fear that immediate violence would be used against him".

Section 75(2)(b): Where "any person was, at the time of the relevant act or immediately before it began, causing the complainant to fear that violence was being used or that immediate violence would be used against any person".

Section 75(2)(c): Where "the complainant was, and the defendant was not, unlawfully detained" at the relevant time.

Section 75(2)(d): Where "the complainant was asleep or otherwise unconscious" at the relevant time.

Section 75(2)(e): Where "because of the complainant's physical disability, the complainant would not have been able to communicate to the defendant whether the complainant consented" at the relevant time.

Section 75(2)(f): Where "any person had administered to or caused to be taken by the complainant, without the complainant's consent, a substance which, having regard to when it was administered or taken, was capable of causing or enabling the complainant to be stupefied or overpowered" at the relevant time.

Rape: The Fault Element

Key Principle: **The fault element of rape is satisfied by proof that the defendant intentionally penetrates without reasonable belief that the complainant is consenting. (*Sexual Offences Act 2003*, s.1(1)).**

Commentary

(1) Section 1(2) provides that all the circumstances should be taken into account in deciding whether the defendant's belief in consent was reasonable or not. This includes the steps that he took to ascertain whether there was consent.

(2) Rape has now become a crime of negligence rather than intention or recklessness. This dispenses with the rule laid down in *DPP v Morgan* (1976) (see Ch.2). Whilst it is still the case that an honest mistaken belief is inconsistent with *mens rea* it is no longer the case that liability for rape is restricted to situations where the defendant had *mens rea*. By turning the crime into one of negligence, mistake about consent will still excuse a defendant but only if it is based on reasonable grounds.

(3) Section 76 (above) also provides that the defendant cannot claim that he reasonably believed that the complainant consented where the conditions for subss.(a) and (b) are met. Section 75 (above) provides for an evidential burden on the defendant to rebut the presumption that he did not reasonably believe that the complainant consented where the conditions in subss.(a)–(f) apply.

Assault by penetration: The Actus Reus

Key Principle: **The *actus reus* is committed by the non-consensual sexual penetration of vagina or anus of another person. (*Sexual Offences Act 2003*, s.2(1)).**

Commentary

(1) This creates a new offence to cover those cases of sexual penetration that only amounted to indecent assault under the old law. The offence covers sexual penetration with "a part of his body or anything else" and so can be committed by either sex. As for rape, penetration remains a continuing act.

(2) The meaning of non-consensual is the same as for rape (see above). Where the complainant is aged under 13, liability arises irrespective of consent: s.6. In the case of complainants aged between 13 and 16 (or 18 in the cases of abuse of trust) lack of consent must be proven in order to establish assault by penetration. However consensual acts of penetration may give rise to the alternative charge of sexual activity with a child (contrary to s.9 or s.16 in cases of abuse of trust).

(3) The penetration must be sexual and guidance on the meaning of this term is provided in s.78 (see below).

Key Principle: **Penetration is sexual if a reasonable person would consider it sexual because of its nature. (*Sexual Offences Act 2003*, s.78(a)).**

Commentary

Subsection (a) further provides that in these cases it does not matter what the defendant's purpose is. This is similar to the test under the old law of indecent assault. See *R. v Court* (1989) (below) where Lord Ackner indicated that motive was irrelevant in cases of inherently (unambiguously) indecent assaults. The prosecution did not have to prove an indecent purpose in order to secure a conviction.

Key Principle: **Penetration is sexual if its nature is ambiguous**

but it is rendered sexual by the circumstances and/or the purpose of any person in relation to it. (*Sexual Offences Act 2003*, s.78(b)).

Commentary

(1) This is also similar to the test used in *R. v Court* (1989) to determine the presence of "indecency" in indecent assault. Court had spanked a girl several times across her clothed buttocks. He admitted that the reason for doing so had been a "buttocks fetish". In cases where the assault was not inherently indecent but was objectively capable of being regarded as indecent, the House of Lords held that evidence concerning the defendant's motive or intention could be introduced to determine whether the act was indecent or not. Indecent intention was therefore a necessary element in some cases of "ambiguous indecency".

(2) It also seems likely that the section preserves the decisions in the pre-Act case law which dealt with cases where the act was not inherently indecent (sexual in its nature) and not even objectively capable of being regarded as indecent (because of its nature may be sexual). These cases, for example *R. v George* (1956) and *R. v Thomas* (1985), had held that an undisclosed indecent intention could not render such an assault indecent.

(3) The Act does not provide a definition of "sexual". The definition of "indecent" prior to the Act is clearly not applicable. This had been explained in *R. v Court* (1989) as where "right-minded persons would consider the conduct . . . so offensive to contemporary standards of modesty and privacy as to be indecent". "Sexual" appears to be a broader term than "indecent" and its meaning will need clarification.

Assault by Penetration: The Fault Element

Key Principle: **The fault element is satisfied by proof that the defendant intentionally penetrates without reasonable belief that the complainant is consenting. (*Sexual Offences Act 2003*, s.2(1)).**

Commentary

Section 2(2) provides that all the circumstances should be taken into account in deciding whether the defendant's belief in consent was reasonable or not. This includes the steps that he took to ascertain whether there was consent. Like rape this is a crime of negligence so that a mistaken belief in consent will only exonerate if it is based on reasonable grounds. Sections 75 and 76 (see above) also apply to this offence.

Sexual Assault: The Actus Reus

Key Principle: **The *actus reus* involves a sexual touching without the consent of the person being touched. (*Sexual Offences Act 2003*, s.3).**

Commentary

(1) Touching is defined in s.79(8) as touching "with any part of the body, with anything else [and] through anything". This preserves the gender neutrality of the pre-Act offence of indecent assault. The Act replaces the previous offence of indecent assault although it appears to be more limited in scope. Under the old law, indecent assault could be committed by assault or battery: *Fairclough v Whipp* (1951). Section 3 can be committed by touching (battery) only. The definition of touching is not wide enough to cover cases where the defendant does not come into contact with the complainant but does cause her or him to believe that s/he will. In some cases this conduct might be caught by alternative offence found in ss.4 and 62.

(2) The meaning of non-consensual is subject to the same principles as in rape and the above discussion about the continued applicability of cases such as *R. v Tabassum* (2000) apply equally here. The case law relating to consent, examined in Ch.4, may also be a relevant consideration in cases of sexual assault.

(3) The test for establishing "sexual" is the same as for assault by penetration (see above) and the uncertainties about its meaning are the same.

Sexual Assault: The Mens Rea

Key Principle: **The fault element is satisfied by proof that the defendant intentionally touched without reasonable belief**

that the complainant is consenting. (*Sexual Offences Act 2003*, s.3(1)).

Commentary

(1) In requiring that the touching be intentional, the Act preserves the previous law governing indecent assault: reckless assault was not sufficient, intention was required: *R. v Parsons* (1993).

(2) Section 3(2) provides that all the circumstances should be taken into account in deciding whether the defendant's belief in consent was reasonable or not. This includes the steps that he took to ascertain whether there was consent. This is another of the sexual offences that is satisfied by proof of negligence. This dispenses with the decision in *R. v Kimber* (1983) that honest but unreasonable mistaken belief in consent disproves the fault element. Any mistaken belief must now be based on reasonable grounds. Sections 75 and 76 also apply to this offence.

---

6. HOMICIDE

Actus reus

Key Principle: **The defendant must cause the death of a human being under the Queen's peace.**

Attorney-General's Reference (No.3 of 1994) 1998
With intent to cause her grievous bodily harm, the defendant stabbed a pregnant woman in the abdomen. The child was born prematurely because of the stabbing and died as a result of having been premature.

Held: (HL) Homicide can be charged for causing the death of a child, born alive, by injury inflicted (on the foetus or its mother) prior to its birth. [1998] A.C. 245

Commentary

(1) The position differs if the child is miscarried or still born because a foetus cannot be the object of homicide. Based on the hypothesis that the defendant did not intend to harm

the foetus (or the child that it would become), the House of Lords rejected liability for murder, refusing to apply the doctrine of transferred malice (see p.21). The situation did however give rise to manslaughter (without the necessity of transferred malice), based on the unlawful act of stabbing the mother.

(2) For the principles relating to factual and legal causation, see Ch.1.

(3) The old principle that death must occur within a year and a day of any injury has been abolished by the *Law Reform (Year and a Day Rule) Act 1996*. However, the consent of the Attorney-General is required where more than three years has elapsed between the death and the injury (or where the defendant has already been convicted of an offence in respect of the activity).

Murder: Mens Rea

Key Principle: **Murder requires proof of intention to kill or intention to cause grievous bodily harm.**

R. v Moloney 1985
(see Ch.2, p.16).

Held: (HL) Malice aforethought (the *mens rea* of murder) is only established by proof of intention to kill or cause grievous bodily harm. Recklessness is not sufficient. [1985] A.C. 905

Key Principle: **Intention to kill or cause grievous bodily harm can be established if the defendant foresaw death or grievous bodily harm as a virtually certain consequence.**

R. v Woollin 1998
(see Ch.2, p.17).

Commentary
See also *R. v Moloney* (1985), *R. v Hancock & Shankland* (1986), and *Matthews & Alleyne* (2003) discussed in Ch.2.

Voluntary Manslaughter: Diminished Responsibility

Key Principle: **The defendant must prove an "abnormality of mind" which covers all aspects of the mind's activities, including the ability to control impulses or urges.**

R. v Byrne 1960
A sexual psychopath pleaded diminished responsibility, having killed a woman whilst suffering from violent sexual desires which he could not resist or had difficulty resisting. The judge ruled that such impulses or urges did not fall within the defence.

Held: (CA) Defendant's appeal allowed, manslaughter substituted. Abnormality of mind was "a state of mind so different from that of ordinary human beings that the reasonable man would term it abnormal". There had been a misdirection because this covered not only "perception of physical acts" and "ability to form a rational judgement as to . . . right or wrong" but also "the ability to exercise will-power to control physical acts". [1960] 2 Q.B. 396

Commentary
The court contrasted "abnormality of mind" with the "defect of reason" required in insanity. "Abnormality of mind" was also described in *R. v Thornton* (1992) (see p.58) as covering "capacity to understand", "ability to make sensible, rational judgments" and "ability . . . to exercise control".

Key Principle: **The abnormality of mind must arise from "arrested or retarded development of mind or any inherent causes or induced by disease or injury." (*Homicide Act 1957,* s.2).**

Key Principle: **Where the abnormality may have been caused by a number of factors, the jury should consider diminished responsibility by reference only to factors falling within s.2.**

R. v Gittens 1984
The defendant, who suffered from depression, had been drinking and taking prescribed drugs when he killed his wife and step-daughter. He was convicted of murder and appealed against the direction on diminished responsibility.

Held: (CA) Appeal allowed, manslaughter substituted. Where there is a combination of causes of the abnormality, the jury must disregard the effect of matters (like intoxication) that fall outside s.2, and should only consider the effect of matters (like depression) that fall within s.2. [1984] 1 Q.B. 698

Commentary
Gittens was approved by the House of Lords in *R. v Dietschmann* (2003). Their Lordships held in this case that s.2 did not require the abnormality to be the sole cause of the defendant's acts. The question for the jury was whether "despite the drink, his mental abnormality substantially impaired his mental responsibility". Intoxication is simply ignored in assessing whether the abnormality substantially impaired responsibility.

Key Principle: **The abnormality must substantially impair mental responsibility, which is a question for the jury to decide.**

R. v Byrne 1960
(see p.55).

Commentary
The court suggested that "substantial impairment" might equate, in ordinary language, with "partial insanity" or "on the borderline of insanity". This is criticised in the next case.

Key Principle: **The impairment of responsibility need not be total but must be more than trivial.**

R. v Seers 1984
The defendant killed his wife whilst suffering from chronic depression. He was convicted of murder following a direction

that the test for diminished responsibility was whether he was "partially insane or on the borderline of insanity".

Held: (CA) Defendant's appeal allowed, manslaughter substituted because of a misleading direction. There was sufficient evidence that responsibility had been "seriously" (more than trivially) and therefore substantially impaired. (1984) 79 Cr.App.R. 261

Commentary
The case disapproves the "partial insanity" test suggested in *Byrne*. *Thornton* (see p.58) confirms that "substantial" means "more than mere trivial . . . but . . . not . . . total or absolute impairment".

Voluntary Manslaughter: Provocation

Key Principle: **Things done and/or said are capable of providing evidence of provocation if they cause the defendant to lose self-control.**

R. v Doughty 1986
The defendant was charged with murdering his 17-day-old baby, having lost his temper due to the baby's persistent crying. The judge ruled that "natural episodes or events such as the baby crying could not be evidence of provocation".

Held: (CA) Defendant's appeal allowed, manslaughter substituted. Under s.3 of the *Homicide Act 1957*, provocation was no longer limited to unlawful or wrongful acts. The crying may have caused the defendant's response and so provocation should have been left to the jury. (1986) 83 Cr.App.R. 319

Commentary
Under s.3, most things causing loss of control are capable of being provocation. This includes self-induced provocation: *R. v Johnson* (1989) (see below). Moreover, provocation no longer has to come from the victim nor be aimed at the defendant.

Key Principle: **If there is evidence of provocation, the judge has a duty to leave the issue to the jury even where the defendant does not raise the defence.**

R. v Johnson 1989

The defendant behaved in a threatening manner which caused the victim to attack him. The defendant stabbed and killed the victim and pleaded self-defence but not provocation. He was convicted of murder and appealed that, in the light of the evidence, the judge should have directed on provocation.

Held: (CA) Appeal allowed, manslaughter substituted. The jury rejected self-defence and so could have inferred loss of self-control from the evidence. Therefore the judge had a duty to leave the issue to the jury. [1989] 2 All E.R. 839

Commentary

This is also why provocation should have been left to the jury in *Doughty*. It has since been confirmed that not only must judges direct on provocation but also both counsel have a duty to request such a direction: *R. v Cox* (1995).

Key Principle: **To establish provocation in fact, the defendant must suffer a sudden and temporary loss of self-control at the time of the killing.**

R. v Thornton 1992

The defendant, who had a personality disorder, killed her husband after a history of abuse. They argued and she went to the kitchen, sharpened a knife, and returned to where he lay. He threatened to kill her when she was asleep and she stabbed him. She raised diminished responsibility and the judge also directed on provocation.

Held: (CA) Defendant's appeal against conviction for murder dismissed.

(1) The direction on diminished responsibility was accurate.

(2) There was no misdirection on provocation. Devlin J.'s statement in *R. v Duffy* (1949) that provocation required proof of a "sudden and temporary loss of self-control" was still correct. [1992] 1 All E.R. 306

Commentary

The court maintained that "sudden loss of control" was still appropriate test even where there had been a history of provocation, including domestic violence. This was raised again in *R. v Ahluwalia* (1992) (below) and confirmed in *R. v Thornton (No.2)* (1996). This appeal was based on fresh medical evidence of Thornton's personality disorder and battered woman's syndrome. The Court of Appeal held that this new evidence might be relevant to her defence (see below) and that subsequent case law might mean that her conviction was unsafe and unsatisfactory. Her conviction was quashed and a retrial ordered which subsequently led to a finding of manslaughter.

Key Principle: **The longer the "cooling period" between the provocation and the killing, the less likely that the defence will succeed.**

R. v Ibrams & Gregory 1982

The defendants had been terrorised by the victim for some time and carried out their plan to kill him five days after the last act of provocation. They were convicted of murder after the judge withdrew provocation from the jury.

Held: (CA) Defendant's appeal dismissed. The substantial time lapse between the provocation and the killing, the fact that there was no provoking act just before the killing, and the formation of the plan presented no evidence of loss of self-control at the relevant time. (1982) 74 Cr.App.R. 154

Commentary

The court approved *Duffy* that a "desire for revenge", "time to think, to reflect" suggested no sudden loss of control. However this does not automatically negate provocation; they are simply factors for the jury to consider when deciding the issue: *Ahluwalia.*

R. v Ahluwalia 1992

The defendant killed her husband after years of abuse and violence. He threatened her and when he fell asleep she threw petrol into his room and set fire to it. Charged with murder, she pleaded lack of intent and provocation as alternatives. She was convicted and appealed against the direction on provocation and also because of fresh evidence of diminished responsibility.

Held: (CA) Retrial ordered to consider the evidence of diminished responsibility. The direction on provocation had made it clear that the lack of immediate response did not necessarily disprove the defence but was merely one factor for the jury to take into account. [1992] 4 All E.R. 889

Commentary
In line with *Thornton* and *Ibrams*, the court indicated that the longer the time lapse, the less likely the defence would succeed, but this was ultimately a question for the jury. In *Ahluwalia* the court refused to consider the argument that in domestic violence cases, a time lapse could create a slow-burn reaction rather than an immediate loss of control. Any change in the law was for Parliament not the courts.

Key Principle: **The jury must consider all the circumstances in deciding whether the defendant lost self-control.**

R. v Humphreys 1995
The defendant had been abused for years by the victim. The victim taunted her about a repeated suicide attempt and she thought that he was going to rape her just before she killed him. She was convicted of murder.

Held: (CA) Defendant's appeal allowed, manslaughter substituted. In directing the jury on loss of control the judge should have analysed the various strands of "cumulative" provocation. The defendant's characteristics were also relevant to this issue. [1995] 4 All E.R. 1008

Commentary

(1) This confirms the approach towards cumulative provocation. In deciding on loss of control the jury must consider "the whole picture, the whole story": *Ahluwalia*, *Thornton*.

(2) Factors for a jury to consider therefore include time lapses; any characteristics that may affect the defendant's self-control (see also *R. v Thornton* (1996): battered women's syndrome, personality disorder; and *R. v Morhall* (1996): self-induced addiction); cumulative provocation; and the effect that provocation aimed at others might have on a defendant (see, for example, *R. v Pearson* (1992)).

Key Principle: **The jury must also decide "whether the provocation was enough to make a reasonable man do" as the defendant did. (*Homicide Act 1957*, s.3).**

DPP v Camplin 1978

A 15-year-old boy lost self-control and killed the victim who had sexually assaulted and taunted him. The boy was convicted of murder on a direction that, in deciding whether the reasonable person would have lost control and done as he did, the test was simply the reaction of a reasonable adult. The defendant's appeal was allowed on the basis that the test was that of the reasonable person of the same age as the defendant. The DPP appealed.

Held: (HL) Appeal dismissed. Lord Diplock gave the following direction: "the reasonable man . . . is a person having the same power of self-control to be expected of an ordinary person of the sex and age of the accused, but in other respects sharing such of the accused characteristics as they think would affect the gravity of the provocation to him; and the question is not merely whether such a person would in like circumstances be provoked to lose his self-control but also whether he would react . . . as the accused did." [1978] A.C. 705

Commentary

(1) The case overruled *Bedder v DPP* (1954) (which imposed a purely objective test) and *Mancini v DPP* (1942) (on the requirement of proportionality between the gravity of the provocation and the response of the defendant).

(2) The court excluded from the test characteristics such as exceptional excitability, pugnaciousness, bad temper or intoxication. The particular characteristics in question in the case were sex and age. Other characteristics that the court thought might be relevant included: race; colour; ethnicity; physical infirmity and disability; being impotent or pregnant; and having a shameful incident in one's past.

(3) The decision implied that age was always relevant and many cases did impute the defendant's age to the reasonable person (including mental age as in *R. v Raven* (1982)). However, *R. v Ali* (1989) held that it was unnecessary to allude to the defendant's age (20) because there would be

no difference in the response of a reasonable 20-year-old and that of a person of any other age to the type of provocation in question.

(4) The extent to which particular characteristics of the defendant may be taken into account in applying the objective test is now governed by the next case.

Key Principle: **A defendant's personal characteristics may be taken into account in determining the standard of control that ought reasonably to be expected of the defendant.**

R. v Smith (Morgan) 2001

The defendant suffered from severe depression that affected his ability to control his actions. He stabbed and killed a friend with whom he had spent the evening drinking and arguing. The defendant claimed provocation and appealed against a direction that his depressive illness could only be taken into account when considering the gravity of the provocation but not in deciding whether the reasonable person would have lost self-control. The Court of Appeal allowed his appeal and the Crown appealed.

Held: (HL) Appeal dismissed. By virtue of s.3 of the *Homicide Act 1957*, it was for the jury to decide what the standard of self-control should be in a particular case. It was also for the jury to decide whether the defendant's behaviour complied with that standard. The jury was entitled to take into account any personal characteristics of the defendant in deciding on the gravity of the provocation and also in determining the relevant standard of self-control that could reasonably be expected of the defendant. [2001] 1 A.C. 146

Commentary

(1) Previous case law had determined that personal characteristics of the defendant could be attributed to the reasonable person where the provocation related to that characteristic or where it was relevant to the gravity of the provocation in some other way. For example, in *R. v Morhall* (1996) the defendant was provoked about his addiction to solvent

abuse and the addiction was held to be relevant not only to the question of loss of control but also as a characteristic in the reasonable person test. What was less clear was whether characteristics unrelated to the provocation could also be considered. This question had arisen in particular in relation to mental impairments. This was not problematic in *Raven* because low mental age was treated as equivalent to physical age. A number of Court of Appeal cases such as *Ahluwalia*, *Thornton* (1996) and *Humphreys* seemed to suggest that the characteristic was attributable as such (although in *Humphreys* the taunting related to the characteristic). However, the Privy Council in *Luc Thiet Thuan v R.* (1997) decided that mental impairment reducing control was not relevant to the objective test unless it went to the gravity of the provocation. The importance of *R. v Smith (Morgan)* is that it decides that personal characteristics (including mental impairment) that affect the defendant's ability to exercise self-control may be taken into account even where they are not also relevant to the gravity of the provocation.

(2) The case also makes it clear that a decision about which characteristics are to be considered relevant is entirely a matter for the jury (subject to guidance from the judge). The jury may also take into account other factors or circumstances that they consider relevant as well as any personal characteristics. Although transitory states such as self-induced intoxication will still be excluded from the test, the case decides that both temporary and permanent characteristics that affect the defendant's degree of self-control may be taken into account. In recent cases this has been held to include "jealousy and possessiveness": *R. v Weller* (2003) (CA) and previous good character: *Paria v The Queen* (2004) (PC).

(3) The direction given in *DPP v Camplin* (above) is now amended so that the question is "Whether the behaviour of the accused measured up to the standard of self-control which ought reasonably to have been expected of him" *per* Lord Hoffmann. In answering this question, "the jury may think that there was some characteristic of the accused . . . which affected the degree of control which society could reasonably have expected of him and which it would be unjust not to take into account" *per* Lord Hoffmann.

Involuntary Manslaughter: Constructive Liability

Key Principle: **The defendant must commit the *actus reus* and have any *mens rea* required for the unlawful act which causes the death.**

R. v Lamb 1967

The defendant was convicted of manslaughter, having shot and killed a friend. Misunderstanding how the gun worked, neither the defendant nor the victim anticipated injury.

Held: (CA) Defendant's appeal allowed due to a misdirection. There was no unlawful act (assault) without proof of the *actus reus* and *mens rea*. Since the latter was missing, the offence was incomplete. [1967] 2 Q.B. 981

Commentary

There was no *actus reus* of psychic assault because the victim did not apprehend contact, nor was there physical assault because of lack of *mens rea*. For further examples, see *Slingsby* (see Ch.4) where there was no assault because of consent and *R. v Scarlett* (1993) (see Ch.14, p.168) where there was no assault because the force was used in defence of property.

Key Principle: **The unlawful act must be established as the cause of the death.**

R. v Dias 2002

The victim had died having self-injected heroin from a syringe prepared for him by the defendant. He was convicted on the basis that self-injection was an unlawful act which the defendant had aided and abetted and which had caused death.

Held: (CA) Defendant's appeal allowed, conviction quashed. The act which caused death was the injection and this was not an offence. Without an offence committed by the victim there was no basis on which to find the defendant guilty of an unlawful act as an accomplice. The unlawful act was the supply of the heroin by the defendant but in such a case the jury must be satisfied that it was this which caused the death. [2002] 2 Cr.App.R. 5

Commentary

(1) Injecting the drug into another person is an unlawful act contrary to s.23 of the *Offences Against the Person Act 1861*. An unlawful act can therefore be established where the defendant has actually administered the drug to the victim (as in *R. v Cato* (1976) below and in *R. v Rogers* (2003)). In the latter case, the application of a tourniquet to the victim's arm in order to enable self-injection was held to be the unlawful act of administering the drug (contrary to s.23).

(2) This case establishes that injecting oneself with heroin is not an unlawful act to which a supplier is an accomplice. This casts doubt on the decision in *R. v Kennedy* (1999) (see Ch.1, p.10). However, the court did not dismiss the possibility that a jury may conclude that the chain of causation was not broken by a victim self-injecting.

(3) The court did indicate that it was not possible to rely on possession of the drug as the unlawful act because it was the injection not possession which caused the death. This casts doubt on the *obiter* of the Court of Appeal in *R. v Cato* (1976) (see p.67) that the unlawful act could have been possession of the heroin. However, the decision is consistent with the decision in *R. v Dalby* (1982) where death was caused by self-administration of a drug unlawfully supplied by the defendant. In *Dalby*, the court stated that the supply in itself was not an act which caused direct harm.

Key Principle: **The unlawful act must also be dangerous, in the sense that the reasonable person would realise that it creates a risk of some physical harm, albeit slight.**

R v Church 1966
(see Ch.1, p.13).

Held: (CA) Defendant's appeal dismissed. In the context of constructive manslaughter, the "unlawful act must be such as all sober and reasonable people would inevitably recognise must subject the other person to, at least, the risk of some harm . . . albeit not serious harm." [1966] 1 Q.B. 59

Commentary

Attorney-General's Reference (No.3 of 1994) (1998) (see p.53) makes it clear that the "other person" foreseen as subjected to the risk of harm need not be the ultimate victim. *R. v Dawson* (1985) confirms that the harm foreseen by the reasonable person must be physical. The defendants had committed a robbery at a garage, using, *inter alia*, a replica gun. The 60-year-old attendant suffered from heart disease and died as a result. It was held to be a misdirection to suggest that emotional disturbance was sufficient for the act to be "dangerous". See also *R. v Watson* (1989), which decides that the reasonable person is endowed with any knowledge of the circumstances that the defendant gains in the course of the unlawful act. On the facts, this included knowledge of the victim's age and physical condition.

Key Principle: **The defendant must intend to do the unlawful act but it is not necessary to show that s/he intended or foresaw any harm.**

DPP v Newbury & Jones 1977

The defendants caused the death of a train guard by pushing a paving stone from a parapet onto a train. They were convicted of manslaughter on a direction that it was not necessary to show that they foresaw harm to a person.

Held: (HL) Defendant's appeal dismissed. Constructive manslaughter requires that the defendant intentionally did the act which is unlawful and dangerous. It is not necessary to prove that s/he knew that it was unlawful or dangerous. Moreover, following *Church,* the test for "dangerous act" is objective. [1977] A.C. 500

Commentary

It was held in *R. v Dalby* (1982) that the unlawful act "must be an act directed at the victim and likely to cause immediate injury, however slight". This was originally interpreted as requiring proof that the defendant intended to direct the act at a person. This view was rejected in *R. v Goodfellow* (1986) where it was decided that it was sufficient that the defendant intentionally committed an act which was unlawful, dangerous and caused death. Thus, arson was a sufficiently unlawful act in the case.

Involuntary Manslaughter: Recklessness and Gross Negligence

Key Principle: **Where liability is not based on an unlawful act, the prosecution must prove recklessness or gross negligence.**

R. v Cato 1976

The defendant caused the death of a friend by administering heroin to him with consent.

Held: (CA) Manslaughter by recklessness or gross negligence was an alternative to manslaughter based on an unlawful act. [1976] 1 All E.R. 260

Commentary

Recklessness was described in the case as a "perfectly simple English word". In *Goodfellow*, the court referred to the subjective element of recklessness in manslaughter ("appreciating a risk"). However, there is some doubt as to the nature of risk to be foreseen. Certainly foresight of death (or grievous bodily harm) should be sufficient but so too might foresight of less serious physical injury.

R. v Adomako 1995

An anaesthetist failed to notice that a tube supplying oxygen to a patient had become disconnected during an operation. The patient died as a result. The anaesthetist was convicted of manslaughter and appealed.

Held: (HL) In such cases, it is necessary to prove that the breach of a duty of care caused the death and that, in all the circumstances, the breach was so grossly negligent as to be characterised as criminal. [1995] 1 A.C. 171

Commentary

(1) In order to amount to gross negligence, the court required that there be a risk of death run by the defendant. In *R. v Singh (Gurphal)* (1999) the defendant, who helped his father run a lodging house, was found guilty of manslaughter when a lodger died from carbon monoxide poisoning. He was guilty because he was aware of the danger posed by

a defective gas fire in the house but had failed to take reasonable care to deal with it. The Court of Appeal confirmed that gross negligence involves proof that "a reasonably prudent person would have foreseen a serious and obvious risk . . of death" *per* Schiemann J.

(2) The test for gross negligence is entirely objective and does not depend on proof of subjective recklessness: *Attorney-General's Reference (No.2 of 1999) (2000)* (CA). However, proof of subjective recklessness might be relevant in deciding on the grossness and criminality of the conduct: *R. v Director of Public Prosecutions Ex p. Jones* (2000); *Attorney-General's Reference (No.2 of 1999) (2000)*.

(3) The decision in *R. v Wacker* (2003) establishes that the tortious principle of *ex turpi causa non oritur actio* does not apply to gross negligence manslaughter. The defendant had attempted to smuggle 60 Chinese people into the UK in his lorry. He had sealed the only air vent in order to avoid detection and 58 of the immigrants died. The Court of Appeal dismissed his appeal against his conviction for manslaughter. The Court held that the defendant could not argue that, because they had been engaged in an illegal venture with him, he did not owe the immigrants a duty of care.

---

7. THEFT

Appropriation

Key Principle: **Appropriation is "Any assumption by a person of the rights of an owner . . . and this includes, where he has come by the property (innocently or not) without stealing it, any later assumption of a right to it by keeping or dealing with it as owner". (*Theft Act 1968*, s.3(1)).**

Key Principle: **Appropriation is established by the assumption of any one right of an owner.**

R. v Morris 1984
The defendant swapped price labels on supermarket goods. On appeal against conviction for theft, the question was whether appropriation required an assumption of all of the rights of an owner or whether it was sufficient to assume just one right.

Held: (HL) Appeal dismissed. It was sufficient to prove an assumption of any of the rights. [1984] A.C. 320

Commentary
Acts such as touching or moving goods may therefore be appropriation. However, *obiter*, the House limited its scope by requiring that it be an unauthorised act ("an adverse interference"). This requirement has now been overturned by *DPP v Gomez* (1993) (see p.70).

Key Principle: **Appropriation can occur even though the act is expressly or impliedly authorised or consented to by the owner.**

Lawrence v Metropolitan Police Commissioner 1972
A taxi driver overcharged a passenger (who understood little English). He falsely stated that the offered fare was insufficient and took further monies from the wallet that the passenger held open to him. He was convicted of theft and appealed on the basis that consent prevented liability.

Held: (HL) Appeal dismissed. The facts probably did not establish consent but, in any event, the prosecution did not have to prove that the taking was without consent. [1972] A.C. 626

Commentary
Despite various attempts at reconciliation, there seemed to be a conflict between *Lawrence* and the view in *Morris* that appropriation involves "not an act expressly or impliedly authorised by the owner". Nevertheless, in *Morris*, Lord Roskill agreed that *Lawrence* was rightly decided. He also approved *R. v Skipp* (1975) (CA) where appropriation did not occur until the defendant did an unauthorised act of diverting from his delivery route and *Eddy v Niman* (1981) (DC) where would-be shoplifters were not guilty of theft having done no more than put goods into shop trolleys

(authorised acts). The matter has now been resolved in the next case.

DPP v Gomez 1993

The defendant obtained authority for transactions by falsely representing that stolen cheques were genuine. His conviction for theft of the goods was quashed following *Morris* and the Crown appealed.

Held: (HL) Appeal allowed. It was not possible to reconcile *Morris* and *Lawrence*. *Morris* was incorrect and *Lawrence* should be followed. Therefore the defendant was guilty because appropriation occurred despite consent. [1993] A.C. 442

Commentary

(1) The decision in *Morris* that the assumption of any right amounts to appropriation was approved. Combined with the fact that this can now be consensual or authorised, theft widens yet further in scope because, for example, touching goods on a shop-shelf may now be appropriation. Appropriation may also occur in conflict with the civil law position on rights in property. See *R. v Hinks* (2001) below.

(2) *Skipp* was overruled. Presumably, *Eddy v Niman* is also incorrect because, following *obiter* in *Gomez*, putting goods in a shop trolley may be appropriation.

(3) Following *Gomez*, most cases of obtaining property by deception (*Theft Act 1968*, s.15) are now also cases of theft. Parliamentary creation of a separate offence (s.15) to deal with "consensual" parting with property induced by deception is a strong argument against the decision. For an example of the overlap operating in favour of a defendant, see *R. v Atakpu* (1993).

Key Principle: **Appropriation can occur even where the defendant thereby acquires an indefeasible title to the property.**

R. v Hinks 2001

The defendant received property (in excess of £60,000) from a man of limited intelligence. She was convicted of theft and appealed on the basis that, *inter alia*, she had been given the property as gifts. Since the man was, despite his limited intelligence, capable of making a valid gift, title had passed to her and there could be no theft.

Held: (HL) Appeal dismissed. The definition of appropriation laid down in *DPP v Gomez* (1993) included indefeasible gifts of property. A donee of a valid gift could be said to have appropriated the gift and, if dishonest, may be guilty of theft. [2001] 2 A.C. 241

Commentary

(1) This decision applies *DPP v Gomez* (1993) in that Hinks appropriated even though the victim had consented to parting with the property. However, it also creates a conflict with civil law because she was convicted of stealing property that she was entitled to keep in civil law, having acquired title to it.

(2) The case also clarifies earlier doubts (see for example *R. v Mazo* (1997)) about whether the decision in *DPP v Gomez* (1993) was restricted to situations where consent was obtained by deception. There is no such restriction on its operation.

Key Principle: **If property is stolen once, it cannot be appropriated again by the same person exercising rights over it.**

R. v Atakpu 1993
The defendants hired vehicles abroad by deception and delivered them to Dover, intending to ring and sell them in England. They were convicted of conspiracy to steal (which required proof that the cars were stolen in England).

Held: (CA) Defendant's appeal allowed. By virtue of *Gomez* (HL), the obtaining of the cars abroad by deception was also theft. Since it was not possible for the stolen cars to be stolen again by the same thieves, there was no theft in England. [1993] 4 All E.R. 215

Commentary
Theft Act 1968, s.3 says that a later assumption amounts to appropriation where the person has "come by the property . . .

without stealing it". This precluded the possibility of appropriation by the same person's later assumption of property already acquired by theft.

Key Principle: **Appropriation can be a continuous act but only for as long as the defendant is acting in the course of the same transaction.**

R. v Atakpu 1993
(see above).

Held: (CA) The second ground for allowing the appeal was that the theft abroad did not continue in England (by retention after the hire period or by ringing the cars). The court agreed that appropriation can occur instantaneously (*R. v Pitham & Hehl* (1976) see below and Ch.9, p.100) or it can continue for as long as "the thief can sensibly be regarded as in the act of stealing" (*R. v Hale* (1978), see Ch.9, p.99). However, it could not be said that theft of the cars continued for days after they had first been taken. [1993] 4 All E.R. 215

Key Principle: **Appropriation can occur without coming into possession or contact with the property.**

R. v Pitham & Hehl 1976
The two defendants bought furniture from M (to whom it did not belong) and arrived to collect it. They were convicted of handling stolen goods and appealed. The question turned on whether M had stolen the furniture before the defendants "handled".

Held: (CA) Appeal dismissed. M assumed the rights of an owner by inviting the defendants to buy the furniture. The appropriation was complete on the offer to sell and so the defendants had handled stolen goods. (1976) 65 Cr.App.R. 45

Property

Key Principle: **"'Property' includes money and all other**

property, real or personal, including things in action and other intangible property." (*Theft Act 1968*, s.4).

Key Principle: **"Money" in a bank account in credit or within an overdraft facility is a "thing in action", capable of being stolen.**

R. v Kohn 1979

An accountant used company cheques to draw money from company bank accounts for himself. In some transactions the account was in credit. In others, it was in overdraft within an overdraft facility limit. In others, it was in overdraft in excess of the limit. The defendant appealed against conviction for theft of the cheques and from the accounts.

Held: (CA) Appeal dismissed in respect of stealing from the accounts in credit and those within an overdraft facility. Where an account is in credit, the debt owed by the bank to the customer is a thing in action. A bank is also obliged to meet a cheque drawn on an account within its overdraft facility. This obligation is also a thing in action, capable of being stolen. (1979) 69 Cr.App.R. 395

Commentary

The court said that appropriation did not occur "until the transaction has gone through to completion". However, since *Morris* and *Gomez*, the offence can occur earlier by simply presenting a cheque. This is confirmed in *R. v Williams (Roy)* (2001) where the Court of Appeal held that presenting a cheque which reduced the victim's credit balance in a bank account amounted to appropriation of that balance (property belonging to the victim). However, where the defendant has no direct control over the account but causes another (for example, the victim) to effect a money transfer there is no appropriation by the defendant: *R. v Naviede* (1997) and *R. v Briggs* (2003) of property belonging to another: *R. v Preddy* (1996) (see p.90).

Key Principle: **There is no property, capable of being appropriated, where a bank account is overdrawn without (or in excess of) an overdraft facility.**

R. v Kohn 1979
(see p.73).

Held: (CA) Appeal allowed in respect of stealing from the accounts overdrawn beyond the agreed overdraft limit. No relationship of debtor/creditor arose and the bank had no obligation to meet cheques drawn on these accounts. Therefore there was no thing in action, capable of being stolen. (1979) 69 Cr.App.R. 395

R. v Navvabi 1986
The defendant used cheque cards, obliging a bank to honour cheques when there were insufficient funds in the account and no overdraft facility. He was convicted of theft from the bank.

Held: (CA) Defendant's appeal allowed. There was no appropriation of identifiable property in which the bank had rights. By using the card, the defendant had done nothing that assumed any rights of the bank to part of its funds. [1986] 3 All E.R 102

Commentary
The defendant should have been charged with obtaining a pecuniary advantage (see Ch.8).

Key Principle: **A cheque is two separate types of property capable of being stolen: a piece of paper and a thing of action.**

R. v Duru 1973
The defendants were convicted of obtaining property (cheques) from the GLC by deception (false mortgage application details).

Held: (CA) Dismissing the appeal, it was established that the cheques were pieces of paper (the cheque form—personal property) and the money represented by the cheque (a thing in action—a legal right to sue on the cheque). [1973] 3 All E.R. 715

Commentary
Whilst it is agreed that cheques represent two forms of property, this case was problematic for two reasons. In relation to the things in action represented by the cheques, *R. v Preddy, Slade & Dhillon*

(1996) (see p.90) overrules *Duru* because, on the facts, it is clear that these did not belong to another. They belonged to the defendants as payees. In relation to the cheques as pieces of paper, there is difficulty with the *mens rea* (see p.82). An alternative position that has been argued is that the cheques are property in the form of a "valuable security".

Key Principle: **Confidential information is not property capable of being stolen.**

Oxford v Moss 1978
A student "borrowed" an examination paper to obtain advanced knowledge of the questions. He was charged with stealing the confidential information (the exam questions) and acquitted on the basis that this was not property capable of being stolen.

Held: (DC) Prosecution appeal dismissed. Confidence is a right over property but not a form of intangible property for the purposes of theft. (1978) 68 Cr.App.R. 183

Commentary
Some forms of intellectual property do fall within s.4 either as "intangible property" (for example a patent) or as a "thing in action" (for example a copyright or trade mark). However, by analogy with *Oxford v Moss*, a trade secret is not property.

Belonging to Another

Key Principle: **Property belongs "to any person having possession or control . . . or . . . any proprietary right or interest . . .". (*Theft Act 1968*, s.5(1)).**

R. v Marshall, Coombes & Eren 1998
The defendants appealed against conviction for theft of underground tickets obtained from passengers and sold at a reduced rate to other passengers.

Held: (CA) Appeal dismissed. The tickets still belonged to London Underground because they retained a proprietary right or interest in them. (1998) 2 Cr.App.R. 282

Commentary
The tickets were treated as tangible property rather than as the chose in action represented by the tickets. A second reason for holding that the tickets belonged to London Underground was the express term on the tickets to that effect.

Key Principle: **Control of land may include control of articles on the land.**

R. v Woodman 1974
The defendants were convicted of stealing scrap metal from a disused site owned by ECC. The site was surrounded by barbed wire and notices, declaring it to be private property and excluding trespassers.

Held: (CA) Defendant's appeal dismissed. ECC demonstrated their control of the site by the steps taken to exclude others and were therefore also in control of articles on the site (whether or not they knew of their existence). [1974] 1 Q.B. 754

Key Principle: **A person with a proprietary right or interest can steal the property from another with possession or control.**

R. v Turner (No.2) 1971
The defendant took his car from a garage without paying for repairs. He was convicted of stealing the car and appealed.

Held: (CA) Appeal dismissed. The trial judge had been correct that, even in the absence of a lien over the car, the garage owner had possession and control of it so it could be stolen from him. [1971] 2 All E.R. 441

Commentary
This has been criticised. Whilst the repairer's lien would give the garage a proprietary right over the car, possession or control did not, in civil law, give the garage a better right to the car than the bailor (Turner) who could retake the goods at any time. Compare *R. v Meredith* (1973) (no theft on removing a lawfully impounded car from police possession).

Key Principle: **Property may belong to someone with an equitable right or interest (other than one "arising only from an agreement to transfer or grant an interest").**

R. v Shadrokh-Cigari 1988

The defendant used bank drafts drawn on money credited to an account by mistake. He was convicted of theft and appealed on the basis that the drafts belonged to him and not the bank.

Held: (CA) Appeal dismissed. Applying *Chase Manhattan Bank v Israel-British Bank* (1981), a person paying money under mistake of fact retained an equitable interest in the money. Therefore, whilst the defendant had legal ownership of the drafts, the bank retained an equitable interest. The court also referred to s.5(4) (see below) as an alternative method for reaching the same decision. [1988] Crim. L.R. 465

Commentary

The equitable interest arising in *Shadrokh* is, presumably, because the law imposes a constructive trust and so the decision in *Attorney-General's Reference (No.1 of 1985)* (see p.79) may now be doubted.

Key Principle: **Generally, if possession, control and the proprietary right and interest in goods pass to the defendant before the appropriation, the property does not belong to another.**

Dip Kaur v CC for Hampshire 1981

The defendant was convicted of theft of a pair of shoes. She took a pair which she knew cost £6.99 to the cashier. One was priced at £4.99, the other at £6.99 and the cashier charged £4.99 which the defendant paid.

Held: (DC) Defendant's appeal allowed. Appropriation occurred when she took the shoes from the cashier, having paid the price charged. However, the cashier had acted within her authority and the mistake (which was not about the nature of the goods or identity of the buyer) was not fundamental and so only rendered the contract voidable. Therefore property passed under the contract and the shoes belonged to the defendant when she left the shop. [1981] 2 All E.R. 430

Commentary

(1) The court stated that s.5(4) (see below) was inapplicable because, under a voidable contract, the defendant was under no obligation to restore the shoes unless or until the contract was avoided.

(2) If the mistake had been fundamental the contract would have been void and property would not have passed.

(3) Under *Gomez*, the defendant would probably be guilty because appropriation would occur earlier, whilst the shoes still belonged to the shop.

(4) For other examples of the importance in the timing of property passing see *Edwards v Ddin* (1976) and *R. v McHugh* (1976) (petrol put into a car); and *Corcoran v Whent* (1977) (eating a meal in a restaurant).

Key Principle: **Property belongs to another under *Theft Act 1968,* s.5(3) "where a person receives property from or on account of another, and is under an obligation to the other to retain and deal with that property or its proceeds in a particular way".**

Key Principle: **Under s.5(3), there must be an arrangement giving rise to a legally enforceable obligation to deal with the specific property (or its proceeds) in a particular way.**

R. v Hall 1973
A travel agent was convicted of theft of monies received for flights. He paid the money into the firm's account but did not arrange flights and could not refund the money.

Held: (CA) Defendant's appeal allowed. The defendant was under a contractual obligation to book and pay for flights but there was no "special arrangement" that he retain or deal with that money (or its proceeds) in that particular way. Therefore, there was no obligation to do so and the money did not belong to another under s.5(3). [1973] 1 Q.B. 126

Commentary

(1) A similar conclusion was reached in *DPP v Huskinson* (1988) (receipt of housing benefit payments). However, contrast *Wakeman v Farrar* (1974) where, on receipt of a duplicate DHSS Giro, the defendant was under an obligation, created by written agreement, to return the original if found.

(2) Also consider *R. v Wain* (1993) where money (or its proceeds) collected for the Telethon Trust, paid into a special bank account, was subject to a trust obligation to be dealt with in a particular way. But note the importance of correctly identifying in the charge the party to whom the property is deemed to belong. In *R. v Dyke and Munro* (2001) the Court of Appeal allowed the defendant's appeal against conviction for stealing from the donors to a charity. The defendants were trustees of the charity and had appropriated money that had been collected from donors in the street. The Court held that, under s.5(3), the defendants were under an obligation to the beneficiaries of the trust (not the donors) to deal with the money in a particular way. They should therefore have been charged with stealing from the beneficiaries and not the donors.

Key Principle: **Under s.5(3), the property must be received from or on account of another.**

Attorney-General's Reference (No.1 of 1985) 1986
A manager of a public house had a contract with a brewery only to sell their goods and to pay the takings into their account. He bought beer from elsewhere to make a secret profit.

Held: (CA) The profits were not received "on account of" the brewers. Whilst the defendant had breached his contract and was under an obligation to account to the brewers for the profit he had not received it on their account. [1986] Q.B. 491

Commentary
Note the comment on this case at p.77. It might now be possible to argue that the situation gives rise to a constructive trust (which, even if, as stated in the case, does not fall within s.5(1) does mean

that the profit is obtained "on account" of the beneficiary). Support is drawn from a civil case, *Attorney-General of Hong Kong v Reid* (1994) which holds that a person in a fiduciary position, receiving a bribe, holds the bribe on constructive trust. This would also affect *Powell v MacRae* (1977) which held that a bribe was not received "on account of" an employer.

Key Principle: **Property belongs to another under *Theft Act 1968,* s.5(4) if received "by another's mistake" where the recipient is "under an obligation to make restoration (in whole or part) of the property or its proceeds or of the value there of . . .".**

Key Principle: **For s.5(4), there must be an obligation to make restoration.**

Attorney-General's Reference (No.1 of 1983) 1985
A policewoman's bank account was mistakenly credited by direct debit with wages that she was not entitled to.

Held: (CA) Whilst the policewoman was not under an obligation to restore the thing in action, she was under an obligation to restore its value to her employers. Therefore failure to do so could amount to theft. [1985] Q.B. 182

Commentary
Contrast *Dip Kaur* (see p.77). The obligation arose here under the civil law of restitution (unjust enrichment) due to the employer's mistake. A similar decision was reached in *R. v Davis* (1988) regarding the mistaken payment of a duplicate housing benefit cheque. *Chase Manhattan Bank* (1981) and *Shadrokh-Cigari* (1988) (see p.77) may now render the use of s.5(4) unnecessary in these cases because the payer may retain an equitable interest so that s.5(1) applies. Certainly where a mistake is fundamental, rendering a contract void, there is no need for s.5(4).

Key Principle: **Under s.5(4), the obligation must be legally enforceable.**

R. v Gilks 1972
The defendant was convicted of theft, having refused to return money mistakenly paid to him by a bookmaker.

Held: (CA) Defendant's appeal dismissed. The money did not belong to another by virtue of s.5(4) because a gaming transaction is not legally enforceable and so the defendant was under no obligation to repay the money. However, because of the mistake, ownership of the money never passed to the defendant and so it belonged to another under s.5(1). [1972] 3 All E.R. 280

Commentary
The ground on which the appeal was dismissed has been criticised as incorrect.

Intention of Permanently Depriving

Key Principle: **Intention to permanently deprive is established if the defendant does not intend to return the specific property in question.**

R. v Velumyl 1989
The defendant took cash from his employer's safe, intending to repay the sum borrowed. He was convicted of theft.

Held: (CA) Defendant's appeal dismissed. Intention to return objects of equivalent value might affect the issue of dishonesty but it established intention to permanently deprive of the original objects (the actual currency) taken. [1989] Crim. L.R. 299

Key Principle: **Under the *Theft Act 1968*, s.6(1) intent is present (even without intent to cause permanent loss of the thing) if the intent is "to treat the thing" as one's own "to dispose of regardless of the other's rights".**

DPP v Lavender 1994
The defendant used doors from council property to replace doors in another property, belonging to the same council.

Held: (DC) The defendant had stolen the doors. His intention was to dispose of (deal with) the property regardless of the council's rights. He had therefore intended to treat them as his own. [1994] Crim. L.R. 297

Commentary

(1) This was also the basis for rejecting the appeal in *R. v Marshall, Coombes & Eren* (1998) (see p.75). By re-selling the tickets, the defendants had an intention to treat them as their own to dispose of regardless of London Underground's rights.

(2) In *Lavender*, the court referred to *Chan Man-Sin v Att.-Gen. of Hong Kong* (1988) as authority for the proposition that "to dispose of" included "dealing with". For an alternative view, see *R. v Cahill* (1993) where the court accepted that it meant "to deal with definitely; to get rid of".

Key Principle: **Intent is established where a defendant intends to return the thing once it has ceased, in substance, to be the same thing.**

R. v Duru 1973
(see p.73). One of the grounds for appeal was that there was no intent to permanently deprive the GLC of the cheques.

Held: (CA) Defendant's appeal dismissed. There was intent to permanently deprive of the cheques as things in action ("the right to receive payment"). Moreover, as a piece of paper, the cheque "changes its character completely once it is paid . . . it ceases to be in substance, the same thing as it was before". [1973] 3 All E.R. 715

Commentary
The *mens rea* in relation to the "things in action" is now irrelevant since *R. v Preddy* (1996) (see p.90) overrules this aspect of the case (see p.75) and also *R. v Mitchell* (1993) which applied *Duru*. In *Preddy*, the House of Lords also doubted that the *mens rea* was established in respect of the piece of paper (the cheque form) since this would be returned to the drawer. It is certainly true that the only change in character relates to the thing in action. As a piece of paper, the cheque form is still in substance what it was before.

The suggestion that the cheque be treated as a valuable security might avoid these problems.

Key Principle: **Under s.6(1), an intent is established in cases of borrowing or lending property if doing so "is for a period and in circumstances making it equivalent to an outright taking or disposal".**

R. v Lloyd, Bhuee & Ali 1985
The defendants took films, made master video tape copies, returned the films and sold pirate video tape versions. They were convicted of conspiracy to steal the films which rested on proof of intent to permanently deprive of the films.

Held: (CA) Defendant's appeal allowed. Under s.6, borrowing only suffices if the intent is "to return the 'thing' in a such a changed state that it can truly be said that all its goodness or virtue has gone". This could not be said because the films still retained their virtue and value on return. [1985] 3 W.L.R. 30

Commentary
Because the films had not lost all their virtue, the borrowing was not equivalent to an outright taking or disposal.

Dishonesty

Key Principle: **A defendant is not dishonest if s/he believes s/he has a legal right to deprive the other of the property. (*Theft Act 1968*, s.2(1)(a)).**

Key Principle: **A defendant is not dishonest if s/he believes s/he would have consent from the person to whom the property belongs if that person knew of the circumstances of the appropriation. (*Theft Act 1968*, s.2(1)(b)).**

Key Principle: **A defendant is not dishonest if s/he believes**

that the person to whom the property belongs cannot be found by taking reasonable steps. (*Theft Act 1968*, s.2(1)(c)).

Key Principle: **Where the defendant does not claim a belief falling under *Theft Act 1968*, s.2, the test for dishonesty is whether s/he realised that the conduct would be regarded as dishonest by ordinary people.**

R. v Ghosh 1982

A surgeon claimed fees that he was not entitled to. He was convicted of obtaining property by deception on a direction that dishonesty was to be tested by contemporary standards.

Held: (CA) Defendant's appeal dismissed. Since dishonesty describes a state of mind, it must be established subjectively. The question is whether "according to the ordinary standards of reasonable and honest people what was done was dishonest . . . and if it was . . . whether the defendant himself must have realised that what he was doing was by those standards dishonest". On that test, the defendant was dishonest and so despite the misdirection there was no miscarriage of justice. [1982] Q.B. 1053

Commentary

Although this case deals with *Theft Act 1968*, s.15, it also establishes the test of dishonesty for theft. The test is not purely subjective because a defendant is not judged by their own standard of honest behaviour but rather on their understanding of "ordinary" standards.

---

8. DECEPTION OFFENCES AND MAKING OFF WITHOUT PAYMENT

Obtaining by deception

Key Principle: **There must be a false representation (of fact, law, or present intention).**

R. v Deller 1952
The defendant believed that the car he was selling was subject to a hire purchase agreement but said that it was "free from encumbrances". In fact this was probably true.

Held: (CA) Defendant's appeal allowed. Although the defendant had *mens rea* (believing that his statement was false), the jury was entitled to conclude that the statement was not, in fact, false, so that the *actus reus* was missing. (1952) 36 Cr.App.R. 184

Commentary
Attempting to obtain by deception covers this conduct.

Key Principle: **A deception may be expressed or implied from words or conduct.**

R. v Silverman 1988
A tradesman, who had built up a relationship of trust with the victims, overcharged them for work. He was convicted of obtaining money by the deception that the sum quoted was a "fair and proper" charge.

Held: (CA) Defendant's appeal allowed due to an inadequate direction. The excessively high quotation could, in the circumstances, amount to a false representation: ". . . the appellant's silence on any matter other than the sums charged was . . . as eloquent as if he had said: '. . . we are going to get no more than a modest profit out of this' . . .". (1988) 86 Cr.App.R. 213

Commentary
Since the defendant never expressly stated that the quotation was fair, the deception was implied. Whether or not an excessive quotation amounts to a deception depends on the circumstances. It probably did here because of the relationship of trust.

Key Principle: **An intention to pay before leaving can be implied from the conduct of ordering a meal in a restaurant.**

DPP v Ray 1974
Intending to pay, the defendant ordered a meal in a restaurant. After eating, he decided not to pay, waited until the waiter left

the room and then ran off. His appeal against conviction for evading liability by deception was allowed.

Held: (HL) DPP's appeal allowed. A deception arose from the representation implied on ordering the meal: that he had the "means and intention of paying for it" before leaving. [1974] A.C. 370

Commentary

This representation only applies if an order is "properly provided" which distinguishes *Guildford v Lockyer* (1975) where no liability arose for leaving after the ordered meal did not arrive and an alternative was not acceptable. A similar representation can also be implied, for example, on entering a taxi or booking into a hotel: *R. v Harris* (1976).

Key Principle: **The representation made on giving a cheque is that it will be met on presentment to the bank.**

Metropolitan Police Commissioner v Charles 1977

The defendant backed cheques with his cheque card thereby obliging his bank to meet the cheques although this created an unauthorised overdraft. The defendant appealed against conviction for obtaining a pecuniary advantage by deception.

Held: (HL) Appeal dismissed for reasons given below. On giving a cheque, one represents that it will be honoured on presentment. [1977] A.C. 177

Commentary

The representation is not that there are sufficient funds in the account to meet the cheque but simply that it will be met on the date specified. The same principle was applied to post-dated cheques in *R. v Gilmartin* (1983).

Key Principle: **The representation made on using a cheque or credit card is that one has authority to use the card.**

MPC v Charles 1977

(see above).

Held: (HL) Defendant's appeal dismissed. Whilst the implied representation that the cheque would be met was true (because it was backed by a guarantee card), a second representation was made on presenting the card. This was that the defendant had "actual authority from the bank to make a contract with the payee on the bank's behalf". This was a deception because the defendant was using the card in excess of his authority. [1977] A.C. 177

Commentary
For decisions based on similar principles see: *R. v Lambie* (1982) (see p.89) where presenting a Barclaycard implied authority to use it; *R. v Sibartie* (1980) (see p.95) where waving an underground season ticket at a station barrier implied authority to travel without further payment.

Key Principle: **A false representation may be implied from silence.**

DPP v Ray 1974
(see p.85).

Held: (HL) The representation of intention to pay was true at the time of ordering but became false after the meal was eaten. The original representation had not ended but continued up to and including the point at which it became false. It continued for as long as the defendant remained in the restaurant, "assuming the role of an ordinary customer". [1974] A.C. 370

Commentary
This, in effect, gives rise to liability by omission. For another example of deception by silence/omission see *R. v Rai* (2000) where the Court of Appeal found the defendant guilty for obtaining services (building works) by deception. He had received a council grant to adapt his house to accommodate his infirm mother but then failed to inform the council when his mother died before the building works started. See also *R. v Firth* (1990) (see p.95) where there was no continuing representation but there was a duty to disclose the truth.

Key Principle: **There must be a causal link between the deception and the obtaining.**

DPP v Ray 1974
(see p.85).

Held: (HL) Whether the deception causes the obtaining is a question of fact. Here it did because "the waiter was caused to refrain from taking certain courses of action which but for the representation he would have taken". [1974] A.C. 370

Commentary

(1) It was probably only because the waiter left the room that the court could say that the deception operated on his mind, thereby causing the obtaining.

(2) Lord Morris referred to the diner who does not intend to pay from the outset who could also be charged with obtaining property (the meal) by deception. Presumably, it could also be obtaining a service (the cooking of the meal, etc.). However, in *Ray*, there could be no such charge because the deception arose after eating the meal. This is why the charge was one of evading liability because this was preceded (and caused) by the deception.

Key Principle: **Causation requires proof that the person "deceived" relied on the false representation alleged.**

R. v Laverty 1970
The defendant was convicted of obtaining property by the deception that a car sold was the original car bearing that number plate and chassis number. He appealed against conviction.

Held: (CA) Appeal allowed. There was insufficient evidence that the statement alleged induced the purchase. The buyer's evidence was that he bought the car because he believed the defendant was its owner rather than because of the representation alleged. [1970] 3 All E.R. 432

Commentary

(1) "Reliance" is normally established on the evidence of the person allegedly deceived. It requires proof that s/he would not have acted in the same way if the truth had been known.

Here the evidence suggested that the buyer might have bought the car even if he had known the truth. Contrast *Charles* where causation was established by the casino manager's evidence that he only accepted the cheques because of the card and would not have done so if he had known that the defendant lacked authority.

(2) The importance of the evidence is also illustrated in *R. v Talbot* (1995) (CA). The defendant received housing benefit after giving false details but was entitled to the benefit in any event. Nevertheless, causation was established because the officers testified that they would not have paid her if they had known the truth.

R. v Lambie 1982
The defendant was charged with obtaining a pecuniary advantage by deception, having used her credit card to pay for goods in excess of her credit limit. The Court of Appeal allowed her appeal and the Crown appealed.

Held: (HL) Appeal allowed. The shop manager gave evidence that it made no difference to her whether the defendant had sufficient credit. However, the representation in question was that the defendant had authority to use the card and it was permissible for the jury to infer that had the manager known that this authority was lacking she would not have completed the transaction. [1982] A.C. 449

Commentary
One difficulty in these cases is that the issue of authority makes no difference to a seller who will receive payment in any event. However, the court inferred reliance because otherwise the inference was that the seller admitted participation in the other's fraud.

Key Principle: **The causal link is too remote if the representation is not an operative cause of the obtaining.**

R. v King & Stockwell 1987
The defendants deceived the victim into believing that her trees needed felling. They were convicted of attempting to obtain the felling fee by deception. They appealed on the basis that the

operative cause of any payment would have been the work done not the deception.

Held: (CA) Appeal dismissed. Operative cause was a question of fact, applying the test of "direct connection between the pretence" and the obtaining. On the facts, there was sufficient evidence that the money would have been paid as a result of the lies told. [1987] Q.B. 547

Commentary

(1) The defence relied on *R. v Lewis* (1922) (Assize Ct) where a teacher was appointed after lying about her qualifications. She was not guilty of obtaining property (her salary) by deception because it was held that this was obtained by the work done and not by the deception. The causal link was too remote (although she might, today, be guilty of obtaining the more closely connected pecuniary advantage, the job opportunity). *Lewis* was distinguished because in *King* the deception was more directly linked to receipt of the money. For other cases to compare on causation, see *R. v Clucas* (1949) and *R. v Button* (1900).

(2) Whilst the deception must not be too remote and must be an operative cause, it need not be the sole cause. This is further illustrated in *R. v Miller* (1993) where the Court of Appeal approved *King*, holding that the jury was entitled to conclude that a false representation that a vehicle was a taxi was one (although not the sole) cause of the fare being obtained. This might also assist in explaining the decision in *Talbot*.

Theft Act 1968, s.15—Obtaining Property

Key Principle: **The defendant must obtain "property", "belonging to another" and "intend permanently to deprive" which mean the same as in theft.**

R. v Preddy, Slade & Dhillon 1996
The defendants obtained (and attempted to obtain) mortgage advances from V by deception. The advances were made by telegraphic and electronic transfer and by cheque. They appealed against their conviction under s.15.

Held: (HL) Appeal allowed.

(1) V's accounts in credit were a chose in action belonging to V but the telegraphic and electronic transfers merely caused the accounts to be debited and created a corresponding credit in the defendants' account. The chose in action thereby created only ever belonged to the defendants and not to another.

(2) The chose in action represented by the cheques also belonged to the defendants as payees. [1996] A.C. 815

Commentary

The *Preddy* ruling in respect of cheques has been applied on a number of occasions: see, for example, *R. v Clarke* (2002) (CA). However, in relation to the transfers, the *Theft Amendment Act 1996* now provides that it is an offence to dishonestly obtain a money transfer by deception. The offence only takes place when the debit (and credit) occur so in the case of cheques it will be when the cheque is honoured.

Theft Act 1968, s.16—Obtaining a Pecuniary Advantage

Key Principle: **Obtaining a pecuniary advantage includes being "allowed to borrow by way of overdraft . . .". (s.16(2)(b)).**

Metropolitan Police Commissioner v Charles 1977
(see p.86).

Commentary

(1) The defendant committed an offence under s.16(2)(b) by creating the unauthorised overdraft. "Allowed to borrow" therefore covers "forcing" a bank to create an overdraft by using a cheque guarantee card. This offence should have been charged in *Navvabi* (see Ch.7, p.74).

(2) Section 16(2)(b) also covers taking out insurance policies and annuity contracts or obtaining an improvement of the terms on which allowed to do so.

Key Principle: **Obtaining a pecuniary advantage includes**

being "given the opportunity to earn remuneration or greater remuneration in an office or employment . . .". (s.16(2)(c)).

R. v Callender 1993
The defendant was convicted under s.16(2)(c), having falsely represented that he had particular accountancy qualifications and membership. He appealed on the basis that a self-employed accountant did not fall within the terms "office or employment" because there was no relationship of master and servant between himself and clients.

Held: (CA) Appeal dismissed. "Office or employment" were not restricted to contracts of service but bore their ordinary meaning which covered "employment" as an independent contractor. [1993] Q.B. 303

Commentary

(1) A charge under this section would avoid the problems encountered in *Lewis* since the offence is committed on gaining "the opportunity to earn . . .".
(2) Section 16(2)(b) also covers being given the opportunity "to win money by betting".

Theft Act 1978, s.1—Obtaining Services

Key Principle: **A service is a non-gratuitous benefit conferred by the doing of an act, or by causing or permitting an act to be done.**

R. v Halai 1983
The defendant was convicted of obtaining (and attempting to obtain) services, having used false details to obtain: a surveyor's report and valuation; the opening of a building society's savings account; and an attempt to obtain a mortgage advance.

Held: (CA) The opening of the account was not a service because no benefit was conferred and no payment was made or expected for doing so. The mortgage advance was also not a service. The survey was a service, being both of benefit to the defendant and something for which payment was expected. [1983] Crim. L.R. 624

Commentary

(1) In *R. v Shortland* (1995) (CA), opening bank accounts under false names did not fall within s.1 because there was no evidence adduced that this was to be paid for. The implica-

tion is that had such evidence been presented, it would have been a service. This was approved in *Sofroniou v R.* (2004) where the Court of Appeal dismissed the defendant's appeal against conviction on a number of counts of obtaining services by deception. The Court held that there was sufficient evidence of an understanding that the credit card and bank services obtained by the defendant were to be paid for. Opening and operating the accounts therefore amounted to obtaining a service.

(2) A mortgage advance is now also a service by virtue of s.4 of the *Theft Amendment Act 1996* which provides that loans (to be paid for by interest or otherwise) are services. For another example of a case involving the obtaining of services by deception, see *R. v Rai* (2000) (p.87).

Theft Act 1978, s.2—Obtaining Evasion of Liability

Key Principle: **"Securing remission" under s.2(1)(a) may require proof that the creditor believes an existing debt is being extinguished.**

R. v Jackson 1983

The defendant "paid" for petrol with a stolen Access card. He was convicted under *Theft Act 1978*, s.2(1)(a) and appealed.

Held: (CA) Appeal dismissed. He had secured remission because the trader, having accepted the card, would look to Access and not the defendant for payment. [1983] Crim. L.R. 617

Commentary

(1) The fact that the creditor thought that the card extinguished liability was sufficient to give rise to s.2(1)(a). The argument that the debt actually has to be extinguished was doubted in *R. v Holt & Lee* (1981) (see below).

(2) There could be no charge for obtaining property (the petrol) by deception because the use of the card (the deception) occurred after property had passed.

Key Principle: **"Inducing a creditor to forgo payment" of an**

existing liability under s.2(1)(b) may be committed by persuading the creditor that no liability is owed.

R. v Holt & Lee 1981
The defendants were convicted of attempting s.2(1)(b) by falsely representing that they had already paid the bill for a meal.

Held: (CA) Defendants' appeal dismissed. The three subsections create three separate offences. All of the elements necessary to establish an attempted s.2(1)(b) were present on the facts and so the defendants were rightly convicted. [1981] 1 W.L.R. 1000

Commentary
It is suggested that the defendants were not guilty of s.2(1)(a) because there was no intent on the part of the creditor to remit the liability (having been deceived into believing that it did not exist).

Key Principle: **Inducing a creditor to take a cheque in payment amounts to inducing the creditor to "wait for payment". (s.2(1)(b)).**

R. v Hammond 1982
The defendant "paid" for repairs done on his car by a cheque that he knew would "bounce". He was charged under s.2(1)(b) and *Theft Act 1978*, s.3.

Held: (Crown Ct.): On the facts, the charge under s.2(1)(b) was appropriate. [1982] Crim. L.R. 611

Commentary
Section 2(3) provides that "for the purposes of subsection (1)(b) a person induced to take . . . a cheque . . . is to be treated not as being paid but as being induced to wait for payment". Contrast the position regarding "dud" cheques under *Theft Act 1968*, s.3.

Key Principle: **"Inducing the creditor to forgo or wait for payment" of an existing liability under s.2(1)(b) requires proof of intention to make permanent default.**

R. v Holt & Lee 1981
(see p.94).

Held: (CA) The court noted that s.2(1)(b) required proof of intent to make permanent default which was not the case in subss.(a) and (c). [1981] 1 W.L.R. 1000

Key Principle: **"Obtaining exemption or abatement" under s.2(1)(c) does not require proof of an existing liability and can be committed by omission.**

R. v Firth 1990
The defendant was convicted under s.2(1)(c), having failed to inform hospitals that his patients were private, thereby avoiding treatment charges. He appealed on the basis that deception could not be committed by omission and that, if it could, there was no liability to pay in existence at the time of the deception.

Held: (CA) Appeal dismissed. Since the defendant had a duty to give the information to the hospital, refraining from doing so could give rise to liability under s.2(1)(c). Moreover, since s.2(1)(a) and (b) specify an "existing liability", the fact that Parliament omitted the term from subs.(c) could be regarded as deliberate. Therefore there is no need for an existing liability under s.2(1)(c). (1990) 91 Cr.App.R. 217

Commentary
The defendant used deception to prevent the liability from arising rather than using a deception to avoid an existing liability. Thus he could not have been guilty of either subs.(a) or (b) but could be guilty of (c).

Key Principle: **The three subsections overlap and are not mutually exclusive.**

R. v Sibartie 1983
The defendant was convicted of attempting to commit s.2(1)(c) of the *Theft Act 1978* having deceived ticket collectors into believing that he had paid for the whole of his underground journey.

Held: (CA) Defendant's appeal dismissed. There was an overlap between the three subsections and the fact that this conduct might amount to attempting s.2(1)(b) did not prevent it from also falling under s.2(1)(c). [1983] Crim. L.R. 470

Commentary
The existence of a liability to pay did not prevent s.2(1)(c) from arising because (c) covers both existing and prospective liabilities. Whilst the conduct also amounted to s.2(1)(b), it presumably did not amount to s.2(1)(a) because the ticket collector did not intend to remit liability (having been deceived into believing that there was none).

R. v Jackson 1983
(see p.93).

Held: (CA) *Holt & Lee* had not decided that the three subparagraphs were mutually exclusive and so whilst the conduct in this case amounted to s.2(1)(a), the fact that it might also have amounted to s.2(1)(b) was irrelevant.

Mens Rea of Deception Offences

Key Principle: **The deception must be deliberate or reckless and the obtaining must be dishonest.**

R. v Ghosh 1982
(see Ch.7, p.84).

Commentary
Ghosh establishes the sole definition of dishonesty in deception offences. Both elements of the *mens rea* must be proved separately. Even where a deception is deliberate (despite comments to the contrary in *Ghosh*) it does not follow that the obtaining was dishonest. An illustration is *Talbot* where although the defendant deliberately lied to local authority officers, she could, presumably, have pleaded that she was not dishonest because she believed that she was, in law, entitled to the housing benefit.

Making Off Without Payment

Key Principle: **The defendant must make off (depart) from**

the spot where payment is expected or required for goods supplied or services done.

R. v Aziz 1993
The defendant refused to pay a taxi fare on arrival at his destination and so the driver was driving to a police station when the defendant ran off. He was convicted under s.3 and appealed on the basis that the spot where payment was expected or required was his destination and not from where he had made off.

Held: (CA) Appeal dismissed. "Makes off" involves departing without paying from the place where payment is usually made, which varies from case to case. There was a making off on these facts. [1993] Crim. L.R. 708

Commentary
In this case the making off was without payment for services done (the taxi ride) and the offence covers any legally enforceable provision of services such as the provision of hotel accommodation, *R. v Allen* (1985) (see p.99) and repairs done on a car, *R. v Hammond* (1982) (see p.94). It also covers the supply of goods, such as a meal in a restaurant, in which case, the "spot" varies according to the nature of the restaurant (it might, for example, be at the table or at the exit point).

Key Principle: **The defendant must be required or expected to pay at the time of the making off.**

R. v Vincent 2001
The defendant stayed in two hotels and left without paying the bills. He claimed that the proprietors of the hotels had agreed to postpone the payment. The defendant appealed against conviction for making off without payment.

Held: (CA) Appeal allowed. An arrangement to delay payment, made before payment is normally expected or required, prevents the offence from occurring. It made no difference whether the arrangement was obtained honestly or dishonestly. [2001] 1 W.L.R. 1172

Commentary
Where the agreement is obtained dishonestly, a charge of obtaining services or evasion of liability by deception might be appropriate.

Key Principle: **The expectation (or requirement) of payment must be legally enforceable.**

Troughton v Metropolitan Police Commissioner 1987
A taxi driver was unable to get destination details from a drunken passenger and so drove to the nearest police station. The defendant was convicted of making off without payment of the fare and appealed.

Held: (DC) Appeal allowed. The driver had breached the contract by not completing the journey. Therefore he was not legally entitled to require payment of the fare and so the defendant was not guilty. [1987] Crim. L.R. 138

Key Principle: **The defendant must make off without having paid. There is no such making off if a cheque is accepted in "payment".**

R. v Hammond 1982
(see p.94).

Held: (Crown Ct) The defendant did not make off without payment because the garage accepted the cheque without a cheque guarantee card and allowed the defendant to leave. [1982] Crim. L.R. 611

Commentary
This is a difficult case. Does it decide that the "consent" of the garage prevented a making off or is it that the cheque was "payment"? The judge distinguished the case of counterfeit money on the basis that the recipient does not know that s/he is taking a risk as s/he does with an unbacked cheque. This suggests that it is not the "allowing the defendant to leave" that prevents a making off, because that applies equally to counterfeit money. The dif-

ference is that counterfeit money is not legal tender but a cheque is. Therefore, it might be that a cheque (even a "dud" one) is treated as payment for the purposes of s.3 but not for s.2(1)(b). However, it is hard to see how a "dud" cheque is payment as "required or expected".

Key Principle: **The defendant must intend to make permanent default.**

R. v Allen 1985
The defendant left a hotel without paying his bill but claimed to intend to pay in due course. The Court of Appeal allowed his appeal against conviction and the Crown appealed.

Held: (HL) Appeal dismissed. The reference in s.3 to "intent to avoid payment" means "intention to evade payment altogether". [1985] 1 A.C. 1029

Commentary
The other elements to the *mens rea* of s.3 are knowledge that payment is expected or required and dishonesty (as defined in *Ghosh*).

---

9. OTHER OFFENCES CONTRARY TO THE THEFT ACTS

Robbery

Key Principle: **The defendant must use force on a person or seek to put a person in fear of force immediately before or at the time of stealing.**

R. v Hale 1979
The defendant put his hand over a woman's mouth to prevent screaming whilst the other searched her house. The latter returned with jewellery and the defendants tied and gagged the

woman to make their escape. The defendant was convicted and appealed against the direction that using force to effect an escape was sufficient for robbery.

Held: (CA) Appeal dismissed. It was for the jury to decide, as matter of common sense, when the act of appropriation finished. Therefore it was open for them to decide that robbery occurred when the force was used immediately before or at the time of the theft, which still continued to the time that the victim was bound and gagged. (1978) 68 Cr.App.R. 415

Commentary

(1) The *actus reus* and *mens rea* of theft must be established. In this case, appropriation was a continuing act (compare *R. v Pitham & Hehl* (1976) (see p.72) and *Atakpu* (see Ch.7, p.71)). *R. v Lockley* (1995) decided that *Gomez* (see Ch.7, p.70) had not affected *Hale* and appropriation could still be continuous so that the defendants were guilty of robbery when they used force after taking beer from an off-licence.

(2) The force must be used on a person and not just against property but the person need not be the one to whom the property belongs.

Key Principle: **The meaning of "force" is to be left to the jury.**

R. v Dawson & James 1976
The victim's wallet was stolen by one of three men whilst he was being jostled by the others. The defendant appealed against conviction for robbery on the basis that this was insufficient evidence of "force".

Held: (CA) Appeal dismissed. "Force" has an ordinary meaning and was for a jury to decide. (1977) 64 Cr.App.R. 170

Key Principle: **The force or "threat" must be used in order to steal.**

R. v Donaghy 1981
The defendants threatened a minicab driver into taking them from Newmarket to London. Once they arrived, they stole his money.

Held: (Crown Ct) The jury acquitted, following a direction that the threats must continue until the time of the theft and be used to obtain the money. [1981] Crim. L.R. 644

Commentary
The jury may have decided either that the threat was too remote from the theft or that it was used to get the ride to London rather than "in order to steal".

Burglary

Key Principle: **The defendant must enter a building or part of a building.**

R. v Collins 1973
The defendant appealed against conviction for burglary with intent to rape. He had entered the bedroom of a young woman who he believed to be inviting him in. There was evidence that he had intended to rape her if she did not consent but they had consensual sexual intercourse until she realised that he was not her boyfriend, as she had thought. A crucial issue was whether the defendant had entered the bedroom via the window before or after the woman appeared to be inviting him in.

Held: (CA) Appeal allowed for reasons discussed below. Edmund-Davies L.J. commented that the first element of burglary was that the defendant entered the building in an "effective and substantial" manner. [1973] Q.B. 100

Commentary

(1) Whilst burglary still requires proof that the defendant entered a building or part of a building, the requirement that the entry be "effective and substantial" has been doubted: see *R. v Brown* (1985) and *R. v Ryan* (1996).

(2) The next case considers the meaning of "a building or part of a building".

R. v Walkington 1979
The defendant was convicted of burglary with intent to steal, having been arrested in a department store, searching through a

till, inside a three-sided counter. He appealed on the basis that he had not entered the store as a trespasser.

Held: (CA) Appeal dismissed. The elements of s.9 included entry to part of a building. The physical partition of the counter was sufficient to mark it off as part of a building into which the defendant had entered. [1979] 2 All E.R. 716

Commentary
Theft Act 1968, s.9 creates two offences: entry as a trespasser with ulterior intent (s.9(1)(a)) and entry as a trespasser and commission of an ulterior offence (s.9(1)(b)). Each offence is also divided into two offences, one where it is committed in a dwelling and the other where the building is not a dwelling. Burglary of a dwelling carries a maximum penalty of 14 years: s.9(3)(a); burglary of other buildings carries a maximum of 10 years: s.9(3)(b).

Key Principle: **The entry must be "as a trespasser".**

R. v Walkington 1979
(see above).

Commentary
The case illustrates that whilst entry to the building may not be "as a trespasser", entry into a part of the building (the three-sided counter) for which one has no permission will suffice.

R. v Jones & Smith 1976
The defendants entered Smith's father's house with intent to steal two televisions. They were convicted of burglary under s.9(1)(b) (on the basis of entering the house as trespassers and stealing therein). They claimed that Smith was not a trespasser because he had his father's permission to enter the house.

Held: (CA) Appeal dismissed. Whilst a person with general permission to enter premises would not normally be a trespasser, entry with the sole intention of stealing once inside was entry in excess of permission and so trespass. [1976] 3 All E.R. 54

Commentary
Both s.9 offences require that the defendant enter as a trespasser. The doctrine of trespass *ab initio* does not apply to burglary:

Collins. Therefore exceeding one's licence after entry does not in itself make the entry a trespass. It was the criminal intention of the defendants on entry in *Jones* that destroyed the permission. This may be contrasted with *Collins* (discussed below). Note also that the implication from *Collins* is that permission to enter may come from the occupier or from the victim of the intended or ulterior offence.

Key Principle: **The defendant must know that s/he is trespassing or be reckless as to the trespass.**

R. v Collins 1973
(see p.101).

Held: (CA) Appeal allowed due to a misdirection on the *mens rea*. The defendant must know that he is trespassing or be reckless as to the fact. If the defendant had already "entered" the window before believing that he was being invited in, he was guilty of burglary. If he had not yet entered, he was entitled to the defence that he had not trespassed because he believed that he had consent for entry. [1973] Q.B. 100

Commentary

(1) Note that the *mens rea* must exist at the time of entry if s.9(1)(a) is charged whilst *mens rea* at any point during the commission of the ulterior offence satisfies s.9(1)(b).

(2) *Collins* was referred to in *Jones & Smith* where the court concluded that the boys were trespassers because they knew that they were entering in excess of the permission given. Whilst *Collins* deals with the *mens rea* of the offence, there is a problem in explaining why, like *Jones*, his criminal intent (to rape) did not destroy any permission to enter (in which case it could similarly be said that he knew he was entering in excess of permission). However, whilst the defendants in *Jones* knew that they were not given permission to enter to steal televisions, *Collins* may have believed that he was given permission to enter for sex (although he clearly was not given permission to enter to rape). There are other differences between the cases. The permission in *Collins* was specific—to enter for sex—whilst in *Jones* it was

general—to use the house whenever. Moreover, the criminal intention in *Jones* is described as unconditional whilst that in *Collins* was conditional.

Key Principle: **Under *Theft Act 1968*, s.9(1)(a) the entry must be with intent to steal, inflict grievous bodily harm, rape, or do unlawful damage.**

Commentary
The defendant must intend to commit the offence in question in the building entered as a trespasser. *Collins* and *Walkington* are examples of charges under this section.

Key Principle: **Theft Act 1968, under s.9(1)(b), the defendant must commit the ulterior offence of theft, attempted theft, inflicting or attempting to inflict grievous bodily harm.**

Commentary
Jones & Smith is an example of a charge under this section.

Aggravated Burglary

Key Principle: **The defendant must have a firearm, explosive or weapon of offence at the time of the burglary. (*Theft Act 1968*, s.10).**

R. v Francis 1982
The defendants were armed with sticks, either just before or on entry to a building, which they then discarded. At the time of entry there was no criminal intent but after entry the defendants stole from the house. They were convicted of aggravated burglary on a direction that it was sufficient that they were armed on entry to the house.

Held: (CA) Defendant's appeal allowed. The aggravating article must be present at the time of the burglary. The relevant time under s.9(1)(a), which did not apply on the facts, was at the point of entry. The relevant time under s.9(1)(b), which did apply, was at the time of the ulterior offence by which time the sticks had been discarded. [1982] Crim. L.R. 363

Commentary
The meaning of firearm, explosive and weapon of offence are explained further in *Theft Act 1968*, s.10.

Blackmail

Key Principle: **The defendant must make a demand.**

R. v Collister & Warhurst 1955
Two police officers were charged with demanding money with menaces. One told the other, in the hearing of the victim, that the victim had been importuning him but implied that a report might not be filed. At a following meeting the victim was asked whether he had brought anything with him at which point he handed over money to the defendants.

Held: (CCA) The trial judge had been correct to direct that there need not be an express demand. Demeanour and circumstances might make it possible to imply that a demand was being made (and being backed by threats). (1955) 39 Cr.App.R. 100

Commentary
The offence is complete on making the demand (with menaces). It is not necessary that an oral demand actually be heard or a written one received: *Treacy v DPP* (1971).

Key Principle: **The demand must be accompanied by menaces.**

R. v Garwood 1987
The defendant was convicted of blackmail having made a demand of someone who was timid and more likely to feel menaced than an ordinary person. The judge directed that the victim's timidity did not prevent the finding of a menace.

Held: (CA) Defendant's appeal dismissed. There had been a misdirection but no miscarriage of justice. Threats that might affect the ordinary stable person but which do not affect the victim can still be menaces. Where a threat affects the victim but might not affect a person of normal stability it must be shown that the defendant knew of the likely effect on the victim before it can be said to be a menace. [1987] 1 All E.R. 1032

Key Principle: **The demand must be unwarranted. It will be warranted if the defendant believes that there are reasonable grounds for making the demand and that menaces are a proper means for enforcing the demand.**

R. v Harvey & Others 1981
The defendants were "swindled" in a cannabis deal by the victim. They kidnapped his wife and child and threatened them and the victim if their money was not returned. They were convicted of blackmail and appealed against a direction that the demand could not be warranted because the menaces involved threats to commit criminal acts.

Held: (CA) Appeal dismissed although the direction was not strictly correct. The test was subjective and so the question was whether the defendants believed the menace to be a "proper" (lawful, not criminal) means for enforcing the demand. (1981) 72 Cr.App.R. 139

Commentary
In this case, the defendants probably believed that they had reasonable grounds for making the demand but they failed to satisfy the latter part of the test.

Key Principle: **The demand must be made with a view to gain or intent to cause loss.**

R. v Bevans 1988
The defendant, who suffered a painful medical condition, called a doctor. When he arrived, the defendant, armed with a gun, threatened to shoot him unless he gave a pain-killing injection. The defendant was convicted of blackmail and appealed on the basis that his actions had not been with intent to gain or cause loss.

Held: (CA) Appeal dismissed. *Theft Act 1968*, s.34(2) specifies that the "gain" or "loss" must be in money or other property. The pain killing liquid was property that the defendant was aiming to gain and so the offence was established. (1988) 87 Cr.App.R. 64

Handling Stolen Goods

Key Principle: **The goods must be stolen goods when handled.**

Re Attorney-General's Reference (No.1 of 1974)
Suspecting that goods in a car had been stolen, a police officer immobilised the car and waited for its driver who was then charged with handling stolen goods. The trial judge directed an acquittal on the basis that the goods had been restored to the lawful possession or custody of the police officer and had therefore ceased to be stolen under *Theft Act 1968*, s.24(3).

Held: (CA) Whether or not the goods ceased to be stolen depended on the state of mind of the police officer. If by immobilising the car, he intended to reduce the goods into his possession or control ("take charge of them so that they could not be removed"), they had ceased to be stolen. However, if he simply intended to prevent the driver from driving away before answering questions, he may not have reduced the goods into his possession or control and so they were still stolen. The trial judge had therefore incorrectly withdrawn the question of the purpose of the officer from the jury. [1974] 2 All E.R. 899

Commentary

(1) Other cases on this point include *R. v King* (1938) and *Haughton v Smith* (1975). Goods also cease to be stolen if restored to the person from whom they were stolen.

(2) "Goods" has much the same meaning as for theft and "stolen" means having been the subject of theft, blackmail or *Theft Act 1968*, s.15. They also include goods directly or indirectly representing stolen goods (see *Theft Act 1968*, s.24(2)).

Key Principle: **The goods must be handled "otherwise than in the course of stealing" (*i.e.* after they have been stolen).**

R. v Pitham & Hehl 1976
(see Ch.7, p.72).

Held: (CA) Defendant's appeal dismissed. Since the appropriation (and theft) was complete on offering the furniture for sale, the actions of the defendants thereafter were not "in the course of stealing" and so could be handling. (1976) 65 Cr.App.R. 45

Commentary
Much turns on the duration of appropriation (as in robbery). Here the court rejected the argument that appropriation continued until the furniture was loaded into the van, deciding instead that it was an "instantaneous" act. For other decisions on the issue in a different context see *Atakpu* (see Ch.7, p.71) and *Hale* (see p.99).

Key Principle: **There are two offences of handling. The first consists of receiving or arranging to receive stolen goods.**

R. v Bloxham 1983
The defendant bought a car which he did not know had been stolen. Discovering that it had, he sold it and was convicted of handling by undertaking or assisting in the disposal or realisation of the car for the benefit of the purchaser. He appealed on the basis that his acts had not been undertaken for the benefit of another.

Held: (HL) Appeal allowed for reasons given below. Lord Bridge explained that *Theft Act 1968*, s.22 creates "two distinct offences" of handling, the first being receiving or arranging to receive. [1983] 1 A.C. 109

Commentary
The first handling offence could not be charged because the defendant lacked *mens rea* when he received (bought) the car.

Key Principle: **Receiving occurs when the defendant comes into possession or control of the goods.**

R. v Brook 1993
The defendant's wife found a bag containing stolen cheques and cards. She told the defendant what was in the bag and he

suggested that they put it in his car whilst deciding what to do. He was convicted of handling by receiving and the issue on appeal related to the mens rea of the offence.

Held: (CA) Appeal allowed for reasons given below. Receipt was complete on coming into possession (control) of the goods. This was when, knowing what was in the bag, the defendant told his wife to put it into the car. [1993] Crim. L.R. 455

Key Principle: **The second form of handling is by undertaking or assisting in the retention, removal, disposal or realisation of goods or arranging to do so. This must be done for the benefit of another.**

R. v Bloxham 1983
(see p.108).

Held: (HL) Defendant's appeal allowed. The second handling offence covers four activities committed in one of two ways: the defendant undertakes the activity for another's benefit or another undertakes the activity and is assisted by the defendant. The "other" is limited in the same way in both parts. A purchaser of stolen goods cannot be "another person" (for whose benefit an activity is undertaken) because the act of purchase does not fall into one of the four activities (retention, removal, disposal or realisation). Therefore, although a sale might be a disposal or realisation for the purchaser's benefit, it does not fall within the section. [1983] A.C. 109

Commentary
The four activities are different: retention means "keep possession of . . . continue to have": *R. v Pitchley* (1972) (see p.110); removal means transporting or carrying; disposal covers getting rid of or transforming; and realisation is selling.

Key Principle: **"Assisting in" retention, removal, disposal or realisation requires something done that helps or encourages for the purpose of enabling the specified activity.**

R. v Kanwar 1982
The defendant lied to the police about stolen goods in her home in order to protect her husband who had stolen them.

Held: (CA) Merely using stolen goods (or keeping them in the house) was not sufficient to amount to assisting in their retention. Concealing goods was sufficient and lying to the police amounted to assisting in retention for the benefit of her husband. [1982] 2 All E.R. 528

Commentary

See also *R. v Pitchley* (1972) where, having received stolen money from his son without knowing it was stolen, the defendant paid it into a post office savings account. Having discovered that it was stolen, he left the money in the account which amounted to assisting in its retention for his son's benefit. This case, unlike *Kanwar*, appears to impose liability for assisting by omission.

R. v Coleman 1986

The defendant knew his wife had stolen money from her employers and this was used to cover their expenses and to purchase a flat. He was convicted of assisting in the disposal of the money.

Held: (CA) Defendant's appeal allowed. Simply getting the benefit from the disposal did not amount to assisting in it which required proof of some act of encouragement, agreement or help. [1986] Crim. L.R. 56

Key Principle: **The *mens rea* (knowledge or belief that the goods are stolen and dishonesty) must exist at the time of the act alleged to be the handling.**

R. v Brook 1993

(see p.108).

Held: (CA) Defendant's appeal allowed due to a misdirection relating to the timing of the *mens rea*. If charged with receiving, the *mens rea* must exist at the point of coming into possession (and not any time thereafter). Moreover, the test for belief that goods are stolen is subjective not objective. [1993] Crim. L.R. 455

Commentary

Contrast handling by undertaking or assisting in the four activities where *mens rea* formed at any point during the continuance of doing so is sufficient. Knowledge or belief that the goods are stolen (and not mere suspicion) is required but this is satisfied where a defendant "shuts his eyes to the obvious": *Pitchley*. The doctrine of recent possession and *Theft Act 1968*, s.27(3) can assist in proof of *mens rea*.

Key Principle: **It is also an offence to dishonestly retain a wrongful credit. (*Theft Amendment Act 1996*).**

Commentary
Because an increased credit balance might not be stolen goods, the Act introduces s.24A to the 1968 Act to cover dishonestly failing to take reasonable steps to secure the cancellation of a wrongful credit.

---

10. CRIMINAL DAMAGE AND ARSON

Criminal Damage Act 1971, s.1(1)

Key Principle: **Property belonging to another must be damaged or destroyed. "Damage" includes temporary impairment of property.**

Hardman v CC of Avon & Somerset 1986
Members of CND were convicted of criminal damage having painted figures on a pavement in soluble whitewash. They appealed on the basis that there was no damage because the paint would wash away.

Held: (Cr. Ct): Appeal dismissed. Damage covered "mischief done to property" and, having caused expense and inconvenience to the Local Authority in removing the graffiti, damage had been done. [1986] Crim. L.R. 330

Commentary

(1) "Damage" covers not only permanent or temporary physical damage but also impairment of usefulness or value. See *R. v Whiteley* (1991) (below). Where the damage or destruction is caused by fire, it is arson by virtue of s.1(3).

(2) The property must belong to another: anyone with custody, control, a proprietary right or interest or charge on it: s.10(2).

Key Principle: **The property damaged or destroyed must be tangible but the damage need not be tangible.**

R. v Whiteley 1991
A hacker gained access to an academic network and, *inter alia,* deleted and added files, left messages and changed passwords. He was convicted of damaging the computer discs and appealed on the basis that destruction or alteration of information on discs was damage to intangible property (not covered by the Act).

Held: (CA) Appeal dismissed. The damage done was intangible but the Act does not require tangible damage. The property damaged must be tangible which it was because he impaired the usefulness and value of the discs which were tangible property. The court also referred to the *Computer Misuse Act 1990* which now creates an offence of (and excludes from criminal damage) unauthorised modification of computer material. (1991) 93 Cr.App.R. 25

Commentary
Section 10(1) defines property in much the same way as for theft except that land can be the subject of criminal damage without exception and intangible property cannot. This case decides that damage to intangible property (for example data or computer programs) does not fall within the Act but is included if by so doing the defendant damages tangible property (for example discs).

Key Principle: **The *mens rea* of criminal damage is satisfied by proof of intention or advertent recklessness.**

R. v G 2003
(see Ch.2).

Held: (HL) "A person acts . . . 'recklessly' [within the meaning of s.1 of the 1971 Act] with respect to—

(i) a circumstance when he is aware of a risk that it exists or will exist;

(ii) a result when he is aware of a risk that it will occur; and it is, in the circumstances known to him, unreasonable to take the risk. . . ". [2003] 4 All E.R. 765

Commentary

This decision disposes of the objective test laid down in *R. v Caldwell* (1982). *Caldwell* had defined recklessness as including a failure to advert to an obvious risk. In confining recklessness to subjective advertence, the House of Lords has also disposed of decisions such as *Elliott v C.* (1983) (see Ch.2), *Stephen (Malcolm R.)* (1984), *R. v Sangha* (1988) (see below).

Key Principle: **A defendant who concludes that there is no risk of damage does not commit criminal damage.**

CC of Avon v Shimmen 1987

(see Ch.2, p.20).

Commentary

The case confirms that realising a risk of damage but thinking that it has been minimised amounts to recklessness but mistakenly thinking that there is no risk at all does not.

Key Principle: **Belief that the person entitled to consent to the damage or destruction had consented or would have done so if they had known of the circumstances amounts to lawful excuse. (*Criminal Damage Act 1971*, s.5(2)(a)).**

R. v Denton 1982

The defendant set fire to machinery, having been asked by his employer to do so. He appealed against conviction for criminal damage.

Held: (CA) Appeal allowed. Honest belief that his employer (the person entitled to consent) had consented amounted to a lawful excuse under *Criminal Damage Act 1971*, s.5(2)(a). Moreover, since the owner consented, there was lawful excuse under s.1(1) even without recourse to s.5(2)(a). [1982] 1 All E.R. 65

Commentary

The belief has to be honest but does not have to be based on reasonable grounds. Thus a defendant may rely on this belief where it is caused by self-induced intoxication: *Jaggard v Dickinson* (1981) (see Ch.13, p.147). Nevertheless, a belief, however genuine, that God consented to (or instructed one to do) the damage does not amount to lawful excuse: see *Blake v DPP* (1993) (DC) where a vicar unsuccessfully tried, *inter alia*, to use this defence, having written a Biblical quote on a pillar in protest about the use of military force in the Gulf.

Key Principle: **A defendant has lawful excuse under s.5(2)(b), if the damage was done to protect other property that the defendant believed to be in immediate need of protection and in the belief that the means adopted were reasonable in the circumstances.**

R. v Hill & Hall 1989

Members of CND were convicted under *Criminal Damage Act 1971*, s.3 for being in possession of a hacksaw blade, intending to use it to cut through the perimeter fence of a US base. They claimed the lawful excuse that they were aiming to protect property in the UK from the risk of a nuclear strike by "persuading" the US to withdraw their base.

Held: (CA) Application for leave to appeal refused. The defendant's belief was subjectively judged, but, on the facts as the defendant believed them to be, the action must be objectively capable of protecting property. It was not so here because the actions taken were too remote from that eventual aim. Moreover, the section requires that the defendant believes that the property is in immediate need of protection and there was no evidence that the defendants believed that the nuclear threat was immediate. (1989) 89 Cr.App.R. 74

Commentary

(1) The same conclusion was reached in *Blake v DPP* (1993) (above) where the vicar also unsuccessfully pleaded that his actions were done to protect property in the Gulf States because the causal link was too remote.

(2) The "thing" to be protected under s.5(2)(b) must be property so this defence did not extend to protecting a child in *R. v Baker & Wilkins* (1997) (see p.167).

Criminal Damage Act 1971, s.1(2)

Key Principle: **The "aggravated" offence under s.1(2) does not require proof of actual endangerment but requires proof of intent to endanger life or recklessness in relation to endangering life.**

R. v Sangha 1988
The defendants caused a fire in a flat which was temporarily unoccupied. Moreover, because of the way the buildings were constructed there was no danger of the fire spreading to other flats. The defendants were convicted of criminal damage (arson) contrary to s.1(2) on the basis of recklessness as to whether life would be endangered. They appealed on the ground that (albeit unknown to them) there was no obvious risk of endangerment due to factors that prevented a risk from materialising.

Held: (CA) Appeal dismissed. Section 1(2) did not require that an actual danger to life existed. It was sufficient that the defendants intended such a danger or were reckless about it. For reasons given below, the defendants had been reckless and so the offence was established. [1988] 2 All E.R. 385

Commentary
This was a case of criminal damage contrary to s.1(2), committed by fire. Such cases are charged as arson: s.1(3). The finding of recklessness in *Sangha* was based on an application of the *R. v Caldwell* (1982) objective test for inadvertence. The question in the case was therefore whether the defendants had failed to give thought to a risk that would have been obvious to a reasonable person. The court held that such a person was not to be endowed with "expert knowledge" (about, for example, the construction of the flats). Therefore the defendants had been reckless using a purely objective test. Assuming that the decision in *R. v G* (2003) is not restricted to s.1 of the *Criminal Damage Act 1971*, this part of the decision is no longer correct since *R. v G* has dispensed with the concept of inadvertent recklessness.

Key Principle: **The intent (or recklessness) must be that the**

damage or destruction of the property be the cause of the danger to life.

R. v Steer 1987

The victims were looking out of their bedroom window when the defendant shot at the window. He was charged with, *inter alia,* criminal damage with intent to endanger their lives or being reckless as to whether their lives would be endangered. His appeal was allowed by the Court of Appeal and the Crown appealed.

Held: (HL) Appeal dismissed. It was not enough to show that the defendant intentionally or recklessly damaged property and intended that life be endangered or was reckless thereto. It was necessary to show that the intent was to endanger life by the damage or that the recklessness was as to whether life would be endangered by the damage. Here, the danger was caused by the shot and not by the damage to the property and so the defendant was rightly acquitted. [1987] 2 All E.R. 833

---

11. INCHOATE OFFENCES

Incitement

Key Principle: **Incitement requires persuasion or encouragement and more than mere suggestion.**

R. v Fitzmaurice 1983

The defendant encouraged B to commit a robbery, described as a "wages snatch", from a woman carrying money from her place of work to a bank in Bow. Unknown to either party, the plan was fictitious. The defendant was convicted of inciting B to commit robbery and appealed against the direction on the meaning of incitement.

Held: (CA) Appeal dismissed. The direction clearly drew attention to the element of persuasion needed for incitement. Because B was in need of money and was being offered reward for taking part, accompanying the suggestion by the implied promise of payment established the requisite persuasion. [1983] Q.B. 1083

Commentary
The second ground of appeal (impossibility) is dealt with below. Incitement may occur even where the suggestion originates from the party incited as long as the inciter then induces or persuades the commission of the offence. In *R. v Goldman* (2001) the defendant responded to an advertisement for pornography. The Court of Appeal held that his offer to buy the material amounted to an attempt to incite the advertisers to distribute indecent photographs.

Key Principle: **The defendant must incite another to commit a crime.**

R. v Whitehouse 1977
The defendant pleaded guilty to inciting his 15-year-old daughter to commit incest with him.

Held: (CA) Appeal against conviction allowed. *Sexual Offences Act 1956*, s.11 established that a girl under the age of 16 was not capable in law of committing incest. Therefore, although there had been an incitement to engage in conduct, that conduct was not a crime by the girl and therefore there was no incitement to commit a crime. [1977] Q.B. 868

Commentary
The prosecution tried to avoid the difficulty by alleging incitement of the girl to aid and abet the man to commit incest on her. However, this fell foul of the principle in *R. v Tyrrell* (1894) (see below). Since the girl belonged to the class protected by the existence of the offence, she could not be guilty of aiding and abetting the offence. Therefore, to incite her to do so was not criminal. The principle from *Whitehouse* remains good law although the activity involved is now criminal by virtue of *Criminal Law Act 1977*, s.54.

Key Principle: **A defendant who belongs to a class protected**

by the existence of an offence cannot be guilty of inciting another to commit that offence against him or herself.

R. v Tyrrell 1894

The defendant was convicted of inciting the crime of having sex with her whilst she was under 16.

Held: (CCCR): Defendant's appeal allowed. Since the purpose of the crime was to protect the girl it could not also lead to her being punished for an offence committed on herself. [1894] I Q.B. 710

Commentary

The same decision was reached on aiding and abetting the offence (see Ch.12). The principle is limited to crimes where the person falls within the specific class protected by the crime.

Key Principle: **The defendant must intend that if the incited does as asked s/he will commit a criminal offence.**

Director of Public Prosecutions v Armstrong 2000

The defendant asked X to supply him with child pornography not knowing that X was a police officer. The defendant was charged with inciting X to distribute indecent photographs of children. The magistrate ruled that there was no case to answer because X had no intention of supplying the material. The prosecution appealed.

Held: (DC) Appeal allowed. It was not necessary to prove that X intended to supply the pornography. It was sufficient that the defendant intended or believed that X would act with the fault required for the offence. [2000] Crim. L.R. 379

Commentary

Two cases were relied upon by the defence. The first was *R. v Shaw* (1994) which appeared to have suggested that the person incited must have parity of *mens rea* with the inciter. This case had been criticised and the court in *Armstrong* declared that it did not provide any general principle. The second case was *R. v Curr* (1968) where the defendant was acquitted of the equivalent of inciting women to commit offences under s.9(b) of the *Family*

Allowance Act 1945. Although the defendant knew that receipt of the family allowance payments was unlawful, the court held that it was also necessary to prove that the women knew this. The case had been taken to create a general principle that a defendant could not be guilty of incitement if the person incited lacked *mens rea*. The court in *Armstrong* declared that *Curr* did not provide any such general principle.

Key Principle: **Impossibility may be a defence to inciting a specific course of conduct but not to inciting a general course of conduct.**

R. v Fitzmaurice 1983
(see p.116). The second ground of the defendant's appeal was that the incited offence (being fictitious) was impossible to commit.

Held: (CA) Appeal dismissed. Since incitement is a common law offence, impossibility is governed by *DPP v Nock & Alsford* (1978) (see p.129). It is therefore necessary to distinguish between a persuasion in general terms and one that is directed to a specific crime and target. The former is not defeated by impossibility whilst the latter is. However, on the facts of the instant case, inciting "a robbery of a woman at Bow" was not impossible and so the issue did not arise. [1983] Q.B. 1083

Attempt

Key Principle: The actus reus **of attempt is not established if the defendant is merely preparing to commit a crime.**

R. v Campbell 1991
The defendant, who admitted intending to rob a post office, was arrested just outside the post office door. He had been observed earlier "lurking around" the post office in motor cycle gear and wearing sunglasses as a form of disguise. He had in his possession a threatening note and imitation firearm. He was convicted of attempted robbery and appealed.

Held: (CA) Appeal allowed. The acts undertaken were mere preparation. (1991) 93 Cr.App.R. 350

Commentary

The court took the view that whilst each case was to be decided on its own facts, it was unlikely that a person could be said to have committed an attempt if he had not even "gained the place where he could . . . carry out the offence".

Key Principle: **The *actus reus* of attempt is established if the defendant has done an act that is more than merely preparatory to the commission of the full offence.**

R. v Jones 1990

The defendant bought guns, shortened one barrel and test-fired them. He packed various weapons in his bag and drove to where the victim was dropping his child at school. He got into the victim's car and asked him to drive, pointing at him the loaded sawn-off shotgun (with its safety catch on). The victim grabbed the gun and threw it out of the car. The defendant was convicted of attempted murder and appealed on the basis that there was no attempt because he had still to remove the safety catch from the gun, put his finger on the trigger and pull it before the full offence could be committed.

Held: (CA) Appeal dismissed. Whilst the acts up to and including arrival at the school were only preparatory, getting into the car and pointing the gun was sufficient evidence of attempt. [1990] 1 W.L.R. 1057

Commentary

According to *Campbell* and *Jones*, "more than merely preparatory" is a question of fact and it is not appropriate to refer to the pre-*Criminal Attempts Act 1981* tests. Guidance is provided in *R. v Geddes* (1996) where the test was whether the defendant actually tried to commit the crime (kidnapping) or merely got ready or equipped to do so. The facts apparently suggested the latter. *R. v Tosti* (1997) provides that acts of preparation are capable of being attempts if they are more than "merely" preparation. Applying the guidance from *Geddes*, examining a padlock of a barn at night, with a car and oxyacetylene equipment hidden nearby, was sufficient evidence of attempted burglary.

Key Principle: **The *mens rea* of attempt requires proof that the defendant intended to bring about any results specified in the full offence.**

R. v Whybrow 1951
The defendant connected an electrical device to a bath, causing his wife to receive an electric shock. He was convicted of attempted murder and appealed against the direction that intention to cause grievous bodily harm was sufficient *mens rea* for attempted murder.

Held: (CA) Appeal dismissed. There had been a misdirection but no miscarriage of justice. Whilst murder is satisfied by proof of intent to cause grievous bodily harm, attempted murder is only satisfied by proof of intention to bring about the full offence (*i.e.* intention to kill). (1951) 35 Cr.App.R. 141

Commentary
Whilst the case is decided on the common law, the same principle applies to statutory attempt: *R. v Millard & Vernon* (1987) (see next principle).

Key Principle: **Even where the full offence is satisfied by proof of recklessness in respect of a result, attempting the offence requires proof of intent.**

R. v Millard & Vernon 1987
The defendants were convicted of attempted criminal damage on a direction that recklessness as to the risk of damage was sufficient.

Held: (CA) Defendants' appeal allowed. The *Criminal Attempts Act 1981* requires proof of intent to commit the full offence. This is the position even where the substantive offence is satisfied by proof of recklessness in respect of a result such as "damage" in the case of criminal damage. [1987] Crim. L.R. 393

Commentary
Even prior to *Moloney* (see Ch.2), attempt required proof of direct intent (aim/purpose) in respect of results: *R. v Mohan* (1976).

Foresight was not equivalent to intent. The same is true under the Act: *R. v Pearman* (1984) although the *Woollin* direction may now apply.

Key Principle: **Where the full offence is satisfied by recklessness in respect of elements (other than any specified result), recklessness in respect of those elements is also sufficient for attempting the offence.**

R. v Khan 1990

The defendants were convicted of attempted rape on a direction that recklessness as to lack of consent was sufficient *mens rea*. They appealed on the basis that attempt required proof of intent.

Held: (CA) Appeal dismissed. The words "with intent to commit an offence" in *Criminal Attempts Act 1981*, s.1 only apply to intent to do the act and to cause any results. Therefore, attempted rape required proof of an intent to have sexual intercourse. However, since recklessness as to lack of consent was sufficient for the full offence, the same is true for attempting the offence. [1990] 1 W.L.R. 813

Commentary

Consider the effect of the *Sexual Offences Act 2003* on this decision.

Attorney-General's Reference (No.3 of 1992) 1994

The defendants were acquitted of attempted aggravated arson, being reckless as to whether life would be endangered on a ruling that intent to endanger life had to be proven.

Held: (CA) Intent had to be proven in respect of the result specified in the full offence (damage or destruction) but since recklessness in relation to endangerment of life was sufficient for the full offence it was also sufficient for attempting the offence. [1994] 2 All E.R. 121

Commentary

The court also held that the *Caldwell* definition of recklessness applied as it did for the full offence. This is no longer correct in the light of *R. v G* (2003). Where recklessness is not sufficient for the full offence, knowledge must be established for attempting the offence.

Key Principle: **Impossibility is no defence to a charge of attempting an offence.**

R. v Shivpuri 1987
The defendant was convicted of attempt to be knowingly involved in dealing with a prohibited drug, having received a suitcase which he mistakenly believed to contain drugs. He appealed on the basis that, *inter alia,* impossibility provided a defence to the charge.

Held: (HL) Appeal dismissed. Since the defendant had the *mens rea* and had committed the *actus reus* of the attempt, he was guilty because *Criminal Attempts Act 1981,* s.1(2) provides that impossibility is no defence. The earlier House of Lords decision in *Anderton v Ryan* (1985) was overruled. [1987] A.C. 1

Commentary
The House of Lords decided in *Haughton v Smith* (1975) that legal impossibility was a defence to attempt (*ratio*) as was physical impossibility (*obiter*). *Criminal Attempts Act 1981*, s.1(2) states that "a person may be guilty of attempting to commit an offence . . . even though the facts are such that the commission of the offence is impossible". Nevertheless, in *Anderton v Ryan*, the House decided that Mrs Ryan was not guilty of attempting to handle a stolen video recorder when it could not be proven that it had been stolen. They decided that s.1(2) merely abolished the defence of physical (or factual) impossibility but had not affected cases of legal impossibility. *Shivpuri* overrules this (although it could be distinguished because Shivpuri intended to commit an offence—importing drugs—whilst Mrs Ryan did not—she merely intended to buy a cheap video recorder). Lord Bridge stated that reasons given to explain *Anderton* (the "doctrine" of "objective innocence" and that of "dominant intention") were not to be used. In particular, the latter contradicted s.1(3) of the Act which provides that a defendant's intention is to be judged by reference to the facts as s/he believed them to be.

Conspiracy: Statutory

Key Principle: **The defendant must have agreed with one or more persons that "a course of conduct shall be pursued".**

R. v Anderson 1986

The defendant agreed to participate in the planned escape of a prisoner. He intended to obtain wire cutting equipment to be smuggled into the prison but claimed to intend to take no further part in the scheme. He appealed against conviction for statutory conspiracy on the basis of lack of *mens rea.*

Held: (HL) In dismissing the appeal for reasons given below, Lord Bridge analysed the elements of the offence. The first element was that there must be an agreement between two or more persons to pursue a course of conduct. [1986] A.C. 27

Commentary

Section 1(1) of the *Criminal Law Act 1977* which replaces most of the common law of conspiracy sets out this requirement, which is the same as for common law conspiracy. The way in which the offences differ relates to the nature of course of conduct agreed upon. Where there are only two parties to the agreement, there are certain situations where no liability arises because, for example, the parties are spouses, or one is a minor or the victim of the intended offence.

Key Principle: **The conspiracy is statutory, where the course of conduct agreed upon would, if carried out, amount to or involve one of the agreeing parties in the commission of an offence.**

R. v Ayres 1984

The defendant agreed to defraud an insurance company by falsely claiming that an insured vehicle and its contents were stolen. The defendant was charged and convicted of common law conspiracy to defraud. He appealed on the basis that the conspiracy was to commit *Theft Act 1968,* s.15 and so should have been charged as statutory conspiracy.

Held: (HL) Appeal dismissed. The charge was incorrectly laid but no miscarriage of justice occurred. The *Criminal Law Act*

1977 provides that agreements that necessarily involve or amount to the commission of an offence by one or more of the conspirators are statutory conspiracies. [1984] A.C. 447

Commentary

The House held that statutory and common law conspiracy were mutually exclusive but this is no longer the case: *Criminal Justice Act 1987*, s.12. An agreement to become an accomplice to an offence may not amount to a statutory conspiracy (since being an accomplice does not amount to a crime as such). In *R. v Hollinshead* (1985) (HL), an agreement to manufacture and sell devices which enabled purchasers to defraud the electricity board amounted to a common law conspiracy to defraud but did not disclose a statutory conspiracy. This may support the view that agreements to become an accomplice do not fall within statutory conspiracy. However, alternatively, it was simply that there was insufficient evidence of an agreement to aid, abet, counsel or procure the purchaser's fraud.

Key Principle: **Only planned consequences fall within the agreed course of conduct.**

R. v Siracusa 1990

The defendant was charged with a conspiracy to import heroin from Thailand and another conspiracy to import cannabis from Kashmir. The defendant appealed against, *inter alia,* a direction on the *mens rea* of the conspiracies charged.

Held: (CA) Appeal dismissed. If conspiracy to import heroin is charged, the prosecution must prove that the agreed course of conduct was to do precisely this and not merely to import a drug. Although the full offence is committed even where the defendant believes the drug to be of a different class, a conspiracy to import heroin (Class A drug) cannot be established by proving an agreement to import cannabis (Class B drug) or vice versa. (1990) 90 Cr.App.R. 340

Commentary

(1) The court noted that, facts allowing, it was acceptable under the 1977 Act to charge just one conspiracy to import prohibited drugs of more than one class.

(2) Only intended consequences fall within the scope of the conspiracy and at least two of the conspirators must know of any circumstances that are specified in the full offence. Recklessness is not sufficient.

Key Principle: **A defendant does not have to intend to play an active part in the agreed course of conduct.**

R. v Siracusa 1990
(see above).

Held: (CA) Because participation in a conspiracy varies, knowledge of "what was going on", combined with an intention to participate in the agreement that others will further the criminal purpose is sufficient. (1990) 90 Cr.App.R. 340

Commentary
Simply intending that others continue with the planned course of conduct, with knowledge that this involves the commission of an offence, is apparently sufficient. Problems were caused by the statement of Lord Bridge in *Anderson* that the *mens rea* of conspiracy required proof that the accused "intended to play some part in the agreed course of conduct in furtherance of the criminal purpose". The court in *Siracusa* explained that this did not mean "play some active part" but could be established in the way indicated.

Key Principle: **The course of conduct must necessarily amount to or involve a crime if the agreement were carried out in accordance with the intentions of the conspirators.**

R. v Anderson 1986
(see p.124).

Held: (HL) Defendant's appeal dismissed. The *mens rea* of conspiracy did not require proof that each conspirator intended the agreement be carried out. Therefore, since the defendant intended to play some part in the agreed course of conduct, he was guilty even though he did not intend that the plan be carried out. [1986] A.C. 27

Commentary

Lord Bridge did not take the 1977 Act to mean that the conspirators had to intend the agreement to be carried out. Nevertheless, he wished to ensure an acquittal for persons entering a conspiracy without any intention of playing a part to bring about the agreed course of conduct (such as those entering with intention to frustrate the conspiracy). This point arose in *Yip Chiu-Cheung v R.* (1995). The defendant agreed to import drugs with a person who unknown to him was a drug enforcement officer who entered the agreement in order to arrange for the arrest of the participants. Relying on the *obiter* in *Anderson*, the defendant argued that there was no conspiracy. The Privy Council held that the case fell outside the exception envisaged by Lord Bridge because the drug enforcement officer did intend to take part in the planned crime (albeit intending to frustrate it). However, there may be a conflict between *Yip* and *Anderson* because the former stated that "the crime . . . requires an agreement . . . with the intention of carrying it out". Yet, *Anderson* seems to suggest the opposite. The fact that *Yip* is a case of common law conspiracy is not sufficient to distinguish the cases.

Key Principle: **An agreement conditional upon a contingency arising may still be a conspiracy.**

R. v Jackson 1985

The defendants were convicted of conspiracy to pervert the course of justice by agreeing to injure their co-defendant if he was convicted at trial. They appealed on the basis that their agreement would not "necessarily" amount to or involve the commission of an offence (as required by *Criminal Law Act 1977*, s.1) because the offence would only be committed if the "victim" was convicted.

Held: (CA) Appeal dismissed. If the contingency arose, carrying out the plan would give rise to the commission of an offence. "Necessarily" did not mean inevitably. [1985] Crim. L.R. 442

Commentary

Contrast the example given by Donaldson L.J. in the case of *Reed* (1982).

Conspiracy: Common Law

Key Principle: **Common law conspiracy to defraud consists of agreeing to dishonestly deprive another of something (including injury to a proprietary right) or to dishonestly cause a public officer to act in contravention of duty.**

R. v Scott 1975

The defendants were convicted of conspiracy to defraud by agreeing to borrow, copy and distribute films in breach of copyright. They appealed on the basis that they had not agreed to deceive anyone (such as the copyright owners).

Held: (HL) Appeal dismissed. A conspiracy to defraud could arise without deception or deceit. To defraud was "to deprive a person of something which is his or to which he is or would or might be entitled and . . . to injure some proprietary right of his . . .". It was also possible to commit the offence without financial advantage being gained or loss caused. [1975] A.C. 819

Commentary

The court also recognised conspiracy to defraud involved in deceiving public officers to act contrary to their duty. The offence requires proof of intention to defraud and dishonesty but not intent to cause economic loss. Common law conspiracy to defraud is preserved by *Criminal Law Act 1977*, s.5(2); and *Criminal Justice Act 1987*, s.12 provides that this may be charged even where the agreement is also a statutory conspiracy.

Key Principle: **Conspiracy to corrupt public morals exists at common law where the conduct agreed upon would not amount to an offence by an individual if carried out.**

Shaw v DPP 1962

The defendants published a "Ladies Directory" containing the contact details of prostitutes. They were convicted of, *inter alia,* conspiracy to corrupt public morals.

Held: (HL) Defendant's appeal dismissed. The offence of conspiracy to corrupt public morals existed at common law. This might include conduct that was not in itself illegal but was calculated to corrupt the public morality. The jury were the arbitrators of what corrupted public morals. [1962] A.C. 220

Commentary
The existence of the offence was confirmed in *Knuller v DPP* (1973) (see below) and is preserved by *Criminal Law Act 1977*, s.5(3)(a). "Corrupting public morals" has been described as something that the jury considers to be "destructive of the very fabric of society": *per* Lord Simon in *Knuller*.

Key Principle: **Conspiracy to outrage public decency exists at common law where the conduct agreed upon would not amount to an offence by an individual if carried out.**

Knuller v DPP 1973
The defendants published a magazine with advertisements for homosexual contacts. They appealed against conviction of conspiracy to corrupt public morals and conspiracy to outrage public decency.

Held: (HL) Appeal dismissed in relation to conspiracy to corrupt public morals and allowed in respect of conspiracy to outrage public decency. A bare majority concluded that the latter offence existed at common law but there had been a misdirection on its elements. "To outrage" meant more than "to offend" or "to disgust" and public "decency" was a shifting standard. Moreover, according to Lord Simon, "public" decency means that the offence must be committed in public. [1973] A.C. 435

Commentary
This offence is also preserved by *Criminal Law Act 1977*, s.5(3)(b).

Key Principle: **Impossibility is a defence to common law conspiracy to engage in a specific course of conduct.**

DPP v Nock & Alsford 1978
The defendants were convicted of conspiracy to produce cocaine. They agreed to obtain cocaine from a particular powder

in their possession which, unknown to them, would not produce cocaine.

Held: (HL) Defendant's appeal allowed. Since the agreement was limited to engaging in a specific course of conduct from which it was impossible to commit the full offence, the defendants were not guilty. The answer might differ if the agreement had been of a general nature (for example, to go into the business of cocaine production) because this agreement would not be rendered impossible just because one powder would not yield cocaine. [1978] A.C. 979

Commentary
Whilst this decision still represents the position at common law, statutory conspiracies are governed by *Criminal Attempts Act 1981*, s.5 which provides that impossibility is no defence.

---

12. PARTIES

Accomplices

Key Principle: **An accomplice is one who aids, abets, counsels or procures the commission of an offence.**

Attorney-General's Reference (No.1 of 1975)
(see p.132).

Held: (CA) Liability as an accomplice (secondary party) arises by aiding, abetting, counselling or procuring and these words probably differ in meaning. [1975] Q.B. 773

Key Principle: **Aiding and abetting requires proof of more than non-accidental presence. There must, in addition, be actual agreement, encouragement or assistance.**

R. v Clarkson & Carroll 1971
The defendants watched a rape but there was no evidence that they agreed to or positively assisted in the crime. They were convicted of rape as aiders and abettors and appealed.

Held: (CMAC) Appeal allowed. In the absence of prior agreement or positive physical assistance, mere presence was insufficient without actual encouragement and intention to encourage. [1971] 1 W.L.R. 1402

Commentary
The court felt that mere presence might, in some circumstances, provide evidence of encouragement and intention to encourage. The next case is an example.

Key Principle: **Evidence of encouragement may arise from a failure to prevent an offence if the defendant had a right to control the principal offender.**

Du Cros v Lambourne 1907
The owner of a car was convicted of driving at a dangerous speed, having failed to prevent the driver from doing so.

Held: (DC) Defendant's appeal dismissed. As owner, he could and should have stopped the driver. Failing to do so when he had a right of control was evidence that he encouraged and approved the activity. [1907] 1 K.B. 40

Commentary
Likewise, failing to act in breach of a duty to do so may provide evidence of aiding and abetting: *R. v Forman & Ford* (1988) (see p.134).

Key Principle: **Counselling requires consensus but not causation. It is sufficient that the principal acts within the scope of the counselling.**

R. v Calhaem 1985
The defendant was charged with murder as counsellor and procurer, having hired a private detective to kill the victim. The detective did so, but in circumstances that suggested no substantial causal link between the counselling and the killing.

Held: (CA) Defendant's appeal dismissed. The word "counsel" does not imply a causal connection. There must simply be contact between the offenders and a connection between the counselling and the offence. Since the killing was done within the scope of the counselling, liability was established. [1985] Q.B. 808

Key Principle: **Procuring does not require consensus but there must be a causal link between the offence and the procuring.**

Attorney-General's Reference (No.1 of 1975)
The defendant surreptitiously laced a friend's drink, knowing that he was about to drive. He was charged with driving with excess alcohol as an accomplice and acquitted on the basis that there was no meeting of minds between principal and accomplice.

Held: (CA) Whilst aiding, abetting and counselling probably require consensus, the same was not true of procuring. Procuring "means to produce by endeavour . . . setting out to see that it happens and taking appropriate steps to produce (it)". There must be a causal link in the sense that the offence would not have been committed in the absence of the procuring. Therefore the facts did raise a case of procuring. [1975] Q.B. 773

Key Principle: **An accomplice must intend to aid, abet, counsel or procure the offence. This is satisfied by proof of voluntary involvement with knowledge of the circumstances.**

National Coal Board v Gamble 1959
A weighbridge operator issued a weight ticket to a driver, knowing that the lorry would be driven overweight. The defendants appealed against conviction on the basis of lack of *mens rea*.

Held: (DC) Appeal dismissed. Supplying "the instrument for a crime or anything essential to its commission" amounts to aiding and abetting if done knowingly with intent to aid and abet. Proof of intent only requires an act of involvement voluntarily done. [1959] 1 Q.B. 11

Commentary

Intent does not mean desire or purpose and liability arises even where the accomplice is indifferent about the commission of the offence. Contrast *R. v Clarke* (1985) where it was held that participation with the sole motive of frustrating an offence did not amount to aiding and abetting.

Key Principle: **An accomplice must have more than a general criminal intention but need not know the details of the offence to be committed.**

R. v Bainbridge 1960

The defendant was convicted as an accomplice, having supplied cutting equipment, knowing that it would be used for breaking and entering. He appealed on the basis that he did not know sufficient details of the planned offence to be an accomplice.

Held: (CCA) Appeal dismissed. A defendant who only knows that an "illegal venture" is planned does not have sufficient *mens rea*. However, one who knows that a crime of the type in question is planned does have sufficient *mens rea* even though the details are not known. [1960] 1 Q.B. 129

Key Principle: **It is not necessary that the accomplice knows the type of crime to be committed as long as the crime falls within the range of crimes contemplated.**

DPP for Northern Ireland v Maxwell 1978

A member of the UVF was convicted in respect of driving to a planned bombing. He appealed on the basis that he did not know the nature of the activity to be carried out by the principals.

Held: (HL) Appeal dismissed. Whilst the defendant did not know precisely what form the attack would take, he did contemplate a limited number of offences (including shooting, bombing and the use of an incendiary device). He was therefore guilty of whichever of these contemplated crimes actually occurred. [1978] 3 All E.R. 1140

Commentary
Viscount Dilhorne and Lord Scarman rejected the criteria used in *Bainbridge* because liability should not rest on categorising activities into types of crimes.

Key Principle: **It is not necessary to prove which party was principal and which was accomplice if the crime is committed in the course of a joint enterprise.**

R. v Forman & Ford 1988
The victim was assaulted by one of two police officers in a cell. The defence submitted that, without evidence that the parties were acting in concert, the failure to identify who actually did the act was fatal.

Held: (Crown Ct) Submission rejected. If it cannot be proved which party committed the assault, both must be acquitted unless there is evidence of joint enterprise in the sense that one did the act relying on the other's encouragement not to intervene or report the offence. [1988] Crim. L.R. 677

Commentary
It was similarly stated in *Chan Wing-Siu v R.* (1985) (see p.136) that the prosecution does not have to prove who was principal or accomplice if the offence arises in the course of a pre-arranged plan or concerted action (joint enterprise).

Key Principle: **An accomplice is not liable for acts which fall outside a joint enterprise.**

R. v Powell & English 1997
In *English,* the joint enterprise was to injure the victim with wooden posts. In the course of the attack, the principal stabbed and killed the victim with a knife which English may not have known he had. English was convicted of murder.

Held: (HL) Appeal allowed. If English did not foresee the use of a knife as a possibility, its actual use fell outside the scope of the joint enterprise. This meant that he could not be guilty of murder or manslaughter. [1997] 4 All E.R. 545

Commentary

(1) Even where the accomplice has the relevant *mens rea* of a crime, s/he is not guilty if it occurs outside the joint enterprise (by an act not intended or foreseen by the accomplice). Much therefore turns on the precise scope of the enterprise. The House of Lords applied *R. v Anderson & Morris* (1966) (CA) that if one party "goes beyond what has been tacitly agreed as part of the common enterprise, his co-adventurer is not liable for the consequences of that unauthorised act". However, Lord Hutton suggested that it might be simpler to apply a test of foresight (discussed under the next key principle).

(2) The case also suggests that where a principal uses a weapon different from but equally dangerous to one contemplated, the accomplice may still be liable. This is explained further in *R. v Uddin* (1998) and *R. v Greatrex* (1998) where it was said that whether or not an action is outside the common purpose is one of degree, so if it is of a "type entirely different" (*Uddin*) or "fundamentally different" (*Greatrex*), it may be outside the enterprise. The use of a weapon is one relevant factor in this test.

Key Principle: **Accomplices are liable for acts which they foresee as possibly arising in the course of a joint enterprise.**

R. v Powell & English 1997
In *Powell* the joint enterprise was to purchase drugs. During the enterprise, the drug dealer was shot and killed by the principal, who Powell knew had a gun which might be used to kill or cause grievous bodily harm. Powell was convicted of murder.

Held: (HL) Appeal dismissed. Participation in a joint enterprise with foresight or contemplation of the possibility of the act was sufficient to give rise to liability for that act. It was not necessary for the accomplice to have the *mens rea* of the crime committed by the principal. Foresight that the principal might carry it out with requisite *mens rea* was sufficient. [1997] 4 All E.R. 545

Commentary
So, for example, it is not necessary that the accomplice intended death or grievous bodily harm for liability to arise in murder. It is

sufficient that s/he realises that the principal might kill with this intent. This was said to be an application of the decision in the next case.

Key Principle: **Where the act falls within the contemplation of the accomplice, the extent of liability depends on what the accomplice anticipated as the outcome of that act.**

Chan Wing-Siu v R. 1985

The defendants were convicted of, *inter alia,* murder occurring in the course of a joint enterprise (armed robbery). The defendants appealed against conviction on the basis that they could only be liable if they foresaw death or grievous bodily harm would probably result.

Held: (PC) Appeal dismissed. Liability arose because the acts occurred within the joint enterprise. Whether the liability was for murder or manslaughter depended on what the accomplice contemplated. If they thought that weapons would only be used to frighten, the crime was manslaughter. If they contemplated that they might be used to kill or cause grievous bodily harm, the crime was murder. It was not necessary that this be foreseen as probable, foreseeing that it might happen was sufficient. [1985] A.C. 168

Commentary

(1) Because liability rests on each party's contemplation, an accomplice can be convicted of a more (or less) serious offence than the principal in respect of the same activity. This was confirmed in *R. v Howe* (1987) (see Ch.14). *R. v Roberts, Day (I) & Day (M)* (2001) is an example of a case where the accomplice was convicted of a lesser offence than the principal. The victim was killed in the course of a joint enterprise and the principal was convicted of murder. Although the principal's act (kicking the victim in the head) was contemplated by the accomplice, he had not foreseen the "murderous state of mind" of the principal. Therefore he could not be guilty of murder but was guilty of manslaughter based on having contemplated the infliction of some (not serious) bodily harm. Another similar example is

R. v Gilmour (2000) which involved killing in the course of a joint enterprise to petrol bomb a house.

(2) *Chan Wing-Siu* like *Powell & English* confirms that it is not necessary to prove that the accomplice had the *mens rea* of the principal offence. *Chan Wing-Siu* decides that liability rests on what the accomplice foresaw that the principal might do. *Powell & English* suggests that it also requires foresight of the principal's *mens rea*. This distinction is crucial when considering whether an accomplice could be guilty of a more serious offence than the principal and it is difficult to see how *Powell & English* can be reconciled with the key principle illustrated by *Cogan & Leak* (1976) (see below) or with the principle laid down in *R. v Howe* (above).

Key Principle: **An accomplice can only be convicted if the *actus reus* of the principal offence is committed.**

Thornton v Mitchell 1940

A bus driver was acquitted of negligent driving but the bus conductor (who was negligent) was convicted as an accomplice.

Held: (DC) Defendant's appeal allowed. If the driver had not driven negligently there was no act that the conductor could be said to have aided and abetted. [1940] 1 All E.R. 339

Key Principle: **An accomplice can be convicted even though the principal is acquitted.**

R. v Cogan & Leak 1976

Leak procured Cogan to have sexual intercourse with Mrs Leak without her consent. Cogan was acquitted of rape because the jury accepted that he believed Mrs Leak was consenting. Leak appealed against his conviction for rape as an aider and abettor on the basis of Cogan's acquittal.

Held: (CA) Appeal dismissed. The *actus reus* of rape had taken place and that was sufficient to convict an accomplice. It was no defence for Leak that Cogan was acquitted due to lack of *mens rea*. [1976] 1 Q.B. 217

Commentary

The same principle applies where the accomplice has committed the *actus reus* but has a defence. A further example can be found in *DPP v K & C* (1997) where two girls were convicted of procuring rape even though the principal might have had the defence of *doli incapax* or lack of *mens rea*. The court noted, *obiter*, that if the principal had been aged under 10, no *actus reus* would have been committed and so the girls would not have been guilty.

Key Principle: **A person who uses an innocent agent to commit the offence is guilty as principal offender.**

R. v Cogan & Leak 1976

(see above).

Held: (CA) In the course of dismissing the appeal, Lawton L.J. indicated that Leak could have been indicted as a principal using Cogan (an innocent agent) as the means to procure the offence. [1976] Q.B. 217

Commentary

This part of the judgment has been criticised on the basis that rape is an offence requiring personal action and cannot be committed by an agent. The same problem does not arise with offences where personal action is not specified.

Key Principle: **An accomplice may avoid liability by effective withdrawal from the enterprise.**

R. v Becerra 1975

The principal committed murder in the course of a joint enterprise to use force during a burglary if necessary. One ground for appeal against conviction as an accomplice was that the defendant had withdrawn from the joint enterprise before the killing occurred.

Held: (CA) Application dismissed. The defendant simply said "let's go" and then ran away just before the killing. Effective withdrawal varies according to the circumstances. By the time this defendant withdrew, he would have had to "repent" in a vastly different and more effective manner (by, for example, physically intervening to stop the stabbing or by warning the victim). (1976) 62 Cr.App.R. 212

Commentary

Where possible, communication of withdrawal should be timely and give unequivocal notice that assistance and aid are withdrawn. So, in *R. v Baker* (1994) (CA), saying "I'm not doing it", passing a weapon back to another, and remaining at the scene was neither unequivocal nor effective withdrawal. However, compare this with a case involving spontaneous violence: *R. v Mitchell* (1999). In *Mitchell* the defendant effectively withdrew from a spontaneous attack when he stopped fighting, threw down a weapon and walked away. Also consider the case of *R. v O'Flaherty, Ryan and Toussaint* (2004) which confirms that withdrawal is a question of fact and degree for the jury to decide upon. In this case, the evidence suggested that R and T had withdrawn from a joint enterprise involving spontaneous gang violence before the fatal blow was struck. R and T had participated in the violence at one location but had not pursued the victim to a second location where death was caused. Therefore R and T were not guilty of murder. O'F was guilty because the evidence suggested that he had not withdrawn. He had participated at the first location and then pursued the victim. Still armed with a cricket bat, he had been present (but not active) at the second location.

Key Principle: **A person falling within the class for whose protection the offence exists cannot be an accomplice to it.**

R. v Tyrrell 1894

(see Ch.11, p.118).

Held: (CCCR) For the same reason that the girl could not be guilty of inciting under age sex against herself nor could she be an accomplice to it. [1894] 1 Q.B. 710

Commentary

The same issue was raised in *Whitehouse* (1977) (see Ch.11, p.117). However, a person who is a victim in a looser sense can be an accomplice to the crime involved.

Vicarious Liability

Key Principle: **The language and object of some offences enables vicarious liability to arise for the acts of an agent or servant acting in the course of employment.**

Coppen v Moore (No.2) 1898
Despite contrary instruction from the employer, goods were sold by false description. The employer was liable vicariously.

Held: (DC) Defendant's appeal dismissed. The effect of the relevant statute was to make masters or principals criminally liable for the acts of servants or agents committed within the scope of their employment. The defendant had therefore sold the goods through his servants. [1898] 2 Q.B. 306

Commentary

(1) The "language, scope and object" of the statute enabled the imposition of vicarious liability which arose even though the acts were unauthorised. Other words that can be similarly construed include "use", "supply", "present" and "keep". *Mens rea* words cannot be extensively construed and so this principle can only be used for strict liability offences.

(2) The parties must, generally, be master and servant or agent and the act must occur in the scope of employment and not as a "frolic of the agent's own".

Key Principle: **A person who delegates the performance of their duty to another will be held responsible for the actions and states of mind of that other.**

Allen v Whitehead 1930
Contrary to the licensee's instructions, the manager of a cafe allowed prostitutes to gather on the premises. The licensee was convicted of an offence under the *Metropolitan Police Act 1839* which required proof of *mens rea*.

Held: (DC) Since the defendant was absent from the premises and had delegated to a manager, that manager's acts and knowledge were imputed to the defendant. [1930] 1 K.B. 211

Commentary
In reaching this conclusion, the court looked to the purpose of the Act and concluded that it would be rendered nugatory if licensees could avoid liability by absenting themselves from premises by appointing a delegate.

Key Principle: **Whether delegation has taken place is a question of fact, requiring evidence of the transfer of authority.**

Vane v Yiannopoullos 1965
The licensee was in a restaurant basement when a sale in breach of license took place elsewhere without his knowledge. The sale was by a waitress and the licensee was originally found guilty of knowingly making the sale in breach of licence.

Held: (HL) Prosecution appeal dismissed. There was insufficient evidence of delegation on the facts. The waitress had not been "left in charge of the premises", "all the effective management" had not been handed over. [1965] A.C. 486

Commentary
The House of Lords expressed distaste for the principle of delegation. The defendant was acquitted because the court felt that delegation required a transfer of the whole of one's authority to another and some felt that it was necessary that the licensee be absent from the premises. However, compare the next case.

Howker v Robinson 1973
A barman made an illegal sale whilst the licensee was in a different bar. The licensee was found guilty of the breach of licence and appealed.

Held: (DC) Appeal dismissed. Delegation was a question of fact and since the barman had been given complete control over the lounge bar, effective delegation had occurred. [1973] Q.B. 178

Commentary
The decision was reached despite the presence of the licensee on the premises which the court said was not a conclusive factor. Moreover, delegation had taken place even though there had not been a transfer of all of the licensee's authority to the barman.

Corporate Liability

Key Principle: **A corporation is identified with its controllers (directing mind and will) such that their actions and states of mind are those of the corporation.**

Tesco v Nattrass 1972

A supermarket manager was responsible for an offence under the *Trade Descriptions Act 1968*. The Company was charged and pleaded a defence under the Act that the manager was "another person" for whom they were not liable. Liability turned on whether the manager was a servant (another person) or someone with whom the corporation could be identified.

Held: (HL) Defendant's appeal allowed. A corporation is vicariously liable for the acts of servants in the same way as a natural employer. However, where the acts (and states of mind) are those of "the directing mind and will" of the company, liability is not vicarious. These persons are identified with the corporation, so that their acts and states of mind are those of the corporation. Because of the management structure of Tesco Ltd, store managers were not such persons and their acts were not acts of the company itself. [1972] A.C. 153

Commentary

The court referred to Denning L.J.'s description in *Bolton v Graham* (1957) (CA) that the "brain and nerve centre" of a company are identified with it whilst the "hands" of the company are not. The court said that normally it was the board of directors, managing director and other superior officers who carry out management functions whose actions are identified with the company. The Privy Council in *Meridian Global Funds Management Asia Ltd v Securities Commission* (1995) suggested a more flexible rule of attribution in a case involving a breach of securities legislation. The purpose of the statute was taken into account in deciding that the acts of officers who were for this purpose acting as the company could be attributed to the company. The traditional principle of identification is reaffirmed in *Attorney-General's Reference (No.2 of 1999)* (2000) (CA) in the context of manslaughter.

Key Principle: **Corporate liability can arise for manslaughter.**

P & O European Ferries (Dover) Ltd 1991
On trial for manslaughter arising out of the sinking of the ferry, Herald of Free Enterprise, the question was whether a company could be liable for an offence such as manslaughter.

Held: (Crown Ct) If the perpetrator of the offence was a human being with whom the corporation could be identified, liability could arise. (1991) 93 Cr.App.R. 72

Commentary
Despite previous doubts, the case confirms that corporate manslaughter can arise under the doctrine of identification. Ultimately P & O were not liable because there was no evidence that a controlling officer had the requisite *mens rea*. Compare *R. v Oll Ltd* (1994) where a leisure company and its managing director were convicted of manslaughter in respect of the death of several canoeists in a trip organised by the company. Gross negligence existed in many aspects of the company activities and the director was identified with the company.

---

13. DEFENCES (1)

Self-induced intoxication

Key Principle: **Self-induced (voluntary) intoxication can be used as evidence to disprove the *mens rea* of specific but not basic intent crimes.**

DPP v Majewski 1977
The defendant attacked a number of people but claimed lack of *mens rea* due to self-induced intoxication through drink and drugs. He was convicted of a variety of assaults on a direction that self-induced intoxication was no defence.

Held: (HL) Defendant's appeal dismissed. Where a crime requires proof of specific intent, lack of *mens rea* due to self-induced intoxication results in an acquittal. However, it is a substantive rule of law that self-induced intoxication is irrelevant and no defence to a crime of basic intent (such as assault). [1977] A.C. 443

Commentary

(1) The principles only apply to voluntary or self-induced intoxication (described as an intoxicant "consciously and deliberately" taken) and only where lack of *mens rea* is pleaded. If *mens rea* exists despite intoxication, the defendant is guilty as charged.

(2) There is a major difficulty in satisfactorily defining specific and basic intent crimes. Approval was given to Lord Simon's definition (from *DPP v Morgan* (1976)): a basic intent crime is one whose definition specifies *mens rea* that "does not go beyond the *actus reus* . . . (the act and its consequences)". A specific (or ulterior) intent crime is one where the "*mens rea* goes beyond contemplation of the *actus reus*". It was also suggested in *Majewski* that a specific intent crime is one that requires proof of some "purposive element" and that a crime satisfied by proof of recklessness is one of basic intent. These definitions are not without difficulty. Examples of specific intent crimes given in *Majewski* were murder and s.18 of the *Offences Against the Person Act 1861* whilst assault, s.20, and manslaughter were crimes of basic intent.

(3) The court accepted that there was no logic in allowing the defence to a specific intent crime but not to one of basic intent. The House of Lords decided that s.8 of the *Criminal Justice Act 1968* had no application in cases of voluntary intoxication and basic intent crimes. This suggests that evidence of intoxication turns basic intent crimes into strict liability so that the prosecution no longer have to prove the *mens rea* at the time of the *actus reus*. The reason given was that voluntary intoxication became an integral part of the crime, supplying the element of recklessness required in crimes of basic intent. This reasoning has also been the subject of much criticism (not least because of the problem of lack of contemporaneity). For an example of an alternative approach see the decision in *R. v Woods* (1981) where the Court of Appeal felt that evidence of voluntary intoxication was irrelevant but that the jury must still consider all the other evidence in order to decide whether the defendant was reckless.

(4) The principle established in *Majewski* has been held to apply only where the intoxication is through alcohol or "dangerous" drugs: see *R. v Hardie* (below).

Key Principle: **A defendant may be convicted of recklessly committing a crime even though s/he was not aware of the risks involved at the time of the *actus reus,* if this is due to voluntary intoxication through alcohol or dangerous drugs.**

R. v Caldwell 1982

The defendant set fire to a hotel and was charged with, *inter alia,* arson contrary to *Criminal Damage Act 1971,* s.1(2). He claimed to have been so drunk that the risk of endangering lives had not crossed his mind. The question on appeal was whether self-induced intoxication was relevant to the charge.

Held: (HL) Self-induced intoxication is relevant to a charge of intentional criminal damage but not where the charge includes recklessness. The fact that the defendant was unaware of the risk of endangering life due to intoxication was no defence since the risk would have been obvious to him if sober. [1982] A.C. 341

Commentary

(1) Lord Diplock held that classifying offences as specific or basic intent was irrelevant. What mattered was the nature of the charge. If the defendant was charged with intentionally damaging the property with intent to endanger life, the defence of lack of *mens rea* due to voluntary intoxication would be available. However, if the defendant was charged with reckless damage being reckless as to the endangerment the defence was lost.

(2) In *Caldwell*, the decision was reached by redefining recklessness rather than by applying the rule from *Majewski*. Although the *Caldwell* definition of recklessness was rejected by the House of Lords in *R. v G* (2003) (see Ch.2), that case did not involve an intoxicated defendant. It seems likely that the law remains the same: if the defendant is unaware of the risk because of voluntary intoxication, s/he

is guilty of any basic intent crime (a crime that is charged as committed recklessly).

Key Principle: **If the effect of an intoxicant is not common knowledge, the prosecution must prove that the defendant knew the risk of its effect before *Majewski* or *Caldwell* can be applied.**

R. v Hardie 1985

The defendant was convicted of arson being reckless as to whether life would be endangered. He claimed to lack *mens rea* due to the effect of valium which he had never used previously. He appealed against a direction that because the valium was taken voluntarily it could not negate the *mens rea* of the crime.

Held: (CA) Appeal allowed. *Majewski* and *Caldwell* are based on the premise that using alcohol or hallucinogenic drugs is reckless because their effects are well known. There is a difference between drugs known to cause aggressive or unpredictable behaviour and sedative or soporific drugs where such a presumption of recklessness is inappropriate. In the absence of evidence that it was generally known that valium might render one "aggressive or incapable of appreciating risks", the defendant could only be convicted if he himself appreciated this risk. [1985] 1 W.L.R. 64

Commentary

The principle from *Hardie* does not apply where the effect of the intoxicant is common knowledge and the defendant simply does not know its strength: *R. v Allen* (1988) (CA) (a case involving home-made wine). Moreover, the outcome depends on the charge and the anticipated effect of the intoxicant. For example, the court opined that taking a soporific drug might be no defence to a charge of reckless driving.

Key Principle: ***Majewski*** **(and *Caldwell*) only apply to pleas of lack of *mens rea*. In deciding whether self-induced intoxication can be used in support of a defence, regard must be given to the law relating to that defence.**

Jaggard v Dickinson 1981
Whilst intoxicated, the defendant mistook a house for that of a friend. She broke a window to gain access and was charged with criminal damage. She pleaded a belief (*Criminal Damage Act 1971*, under s.5(2)) that she would have consent for the damage from the person whose house she thought it was. She was convicted on the basis that such a belief, caused by self-induced intoxication, was no defence.

Held: (DC) Defendant's appeal allowed. The distinction between specific and basic intent was only relevant to pleas of lack of *mens rea* and not to the issue of defences. Section 5(2) only required an honest belief and so even one induced by intoxication could be relied upon. [1981] Q.B. 527

Commentary
Whilst the court accepted that the crime (s.1(1)) was one of basic intent, the defendant admitted an intention to damage property belonging to another and the only question related to the s.5 defence.

R. v O'Grady 1987
The defendant was charged with murder and convicted of manslaughter after killing a friend following a drinking spree. He claimed that the killing occurred in self-defence. He appealed on the basis that his defence should be judged not only on any mistaken belief in the existence of the attack but also on any mistake about the severity of that attack.

Held: (CA) Appeal dismissed. The defendant was not entitled, in any event, to rely on self-defence based on a mistake induced by voluntary intoxication. [1987] 1 Q.B. 995

Commentary
The court held that the distinction between specific intent (murder) and basic intent (manslaughter) was irrelevant because mistake was a separate issue from intent. Self-defence was no defence when induced by an intoxicated mistake. The same reasoning was followed in *R. v O'Connor* (1991) (CA) (although the defendant's conviction for murder was reduced to manslaughter because his intoxication may have affected his *mens rea*). However, following *Williams* and *Beckford* (see Chapters 1, 2, 4 and 14), it is difficult to see why mistaken belief in self-defence is a separate issue from intent. According to these cases, such a plea is

a denial of the *mens rea* of the crime charged which should mean that *Majewski* applies and the belief is relevant to a specific intent charge (for example murder) but not to a basic intent charge (for example manslaughter).

Key Principle: **Where a defendant deliberately becomes intoxicated in order to commit a crime, s/he cannot plead lack of *mens rea* at the time of the crime caused by that intoxication.**

Attorney-General for Northern Ireland v Gallagher 1963
The defendant was an aggressive psychopath, a mental disorder with latent effects which could be brought on by alcohol. He killed his wife having formed the intent to do so and having, possibly, consumed alcohol to get the courage for the crime. In his defence, he pleaded insanity and intoxication.

Held: (HL) Prosecution appeal allowed and murder conviction restored. If a person forms *mens rea* whilst sane and sober and then gets intoxicated in order to commit the crime, s/he has no defence irrespective of whether the crime is one of specific or basic intent. [1963] A.C. 349

Commentary
The case also dealt with insanity. Whilst a disease of the mind (such as delirium tremens) brought on by intoxication might give rise to a plea of insanity, this was not such a case. Here there was a disease of the mind (psychopathy) which did not cause a defect of reason nor prevent the defendant from forming *mens rea*. The intoxication then brought out a defect of reason but because he had previously formed *mens rea*, he could not rely on this self-induced defect of reason to plead insanity.

Involuntary Intoxication

Key Principle: **Lack of *mens rea* due to involuntary intoxication is a defence to crimes of both specific and basic intent.**

R. v Kingston 1995
The defendant committed acts of indecency which he claimed were due to him having been surreptitiously drugged. The

judge directed that he could only be acquitted if the drugs caused lack of *mens rea* at the time of the crime. His appeal was allowed by the Court of Appeal and the DPP appealed.

Held: (HL) Appeal allowed. The trial judge was correct. A defendant who had *mens rea* had no defence simply because involuntary intoxication caused him to lose control or to become less inhibited. However, where involuntary intoxication caused lack of *mens rea* it was a defence to any crime. [1995] 2 A.C. 355

Infancy

Key Principle: **A child under the age of 10 is not criminally responsible. A child over the age of 10 may be found to be criminally responsible. (*Crime and Disorder Act 1998*, s.34).**

Commentary
Prior to the Act there was a presumption of *doli incapax* which applied to children between the ages of 10 and 14. This was a presumption that the child was incapable of committing a crime although this could be rebutted by evidence that the child knew that the act was wrong: *C. v DPP* (1996) (HL). The Act has now abolished this presumption.

Insane and Non-insane Automatism

Key Principle: **A defendant is insane if suffering from a defect of reason, caused by a disease of the mind, so as not to know what s/he is doing or not to know that it is wrong.**

M'Naghten's Case 1843
The defendant suffered from delusions. He was charged with murder, having shot and killed Robert Peel's private secretary.

Held: (HL) To be insane, it must be proved that "at the time of the committing of the act the party accused was labouring under such a defect of reason, from disease of the mind, as not to know the nature and quality of the act he was doing, or, if he did know it, that he did not know he was doing what was wrong." [1843–60] All E.R. 229

Commentary
This test is known as the *M'Naghten* rules. The case also establishes the presumption of sanity.

Key Principle: **A defect of reason requires deprivation of the power of reasoning and does not include retaining, but simply failing to use, powers of reasoning.**

R. v Clarke 1972
The defendant, charged with shoplifting, pleaded lack of *mens rea* caused by confusion and absent-mindedness resulting from, *inter alia,* depression. The recorder ruled that the defence was insanity, because of the mental illness from which the lack of *mens rea* arose.

Held: (CA) Defendant's appeal allowed. Whilst depression might amount to a disease of the mind, the defendant was not suffering from a defect of reason because she "retained her ordinary powers of reason but . . . momentarily . . . acted as she did by failing to concentrate properly . . .". [1972] 1 All E.R. 219

Key Principle: **The defect of reason must cause the defendant to either not know the physical character of the act or to not know that it was contrary to the law.**

R. v Codere 1917
The defendant killed a fellow soldier and was convicted of murder. The defence raised insanity.

Held: (CA) The expression "nature and quality of the act" related to the physical character of the act (not its moral character). Moreover, "not knowing that the act was 'wrong'" meant "wrong in law" or "regarded as wrong by reasonable people". Therefore, a defendant who knew what he was doing and knew that it was contrary to the law was not insane even though he might not understand that the act was morally wrong. (1917) 12 Cr.App.R. 21

Commentary
"Not knowing the nature and quality of an act" means that "he did not know what he was doing": *R. v Sullivan* (1984). Regarding

knowledge that the act was wrong, a similar decision was reached in *R. v Windle* (1952) where the defendant was not insane because he recognised that his act was contrary to the law (even though he may have thought that it was justified).

Key Principle: **A disease of the mind may be any curable or incurable physical or mental disease, of transitory or permanent effect.**

R. v Kemp 1957
A devoted husband struck his wife with a hammer during a temporary lapse of consciousness caused by the effect of arteriosclerosis (hardening of the arteries). Since it was accepted that he did not know what he was doing due to a defect of reason, the only question was whether the cause of the defect fell within the definition of disease of the mind.

Held: (Assize Ct) The defendant was insane because hardening of the arteries was a disease of the mind. The law does not distinguish between diseases of mental and physical origin. Either may amount to a disease of the mind if they bring about the relevant defect of reason. The condition of the brain is irrelevant as is the fact that the condition is curable or incurable, transitory or permanent. [1957] 1 Q.B. 399

Commentary
Any disease that affects the "mental faculties of reason, memory and understanding" falls within the *M'Naghten* rules. The definition given in the case received approval in *Sullivan* (see p.152), subject to the important qualification imposed by *R. v Quick & Paddison* (1973) (see p.152).

Key Principle: **"Any mental disorder which has manifested itself in violence and is prone to recur" may be a disease of the mind.**

Bratty v Attorney-General for Northern Ireland 1963
The defendant was convicted of murder but claimed not to be conscious of his actions due to psychomotor epilepsy. He

appealed on the basis that his defence of automatism should have been left to the jury.

Held: (HL) Appeal dismissed for reasons given below. Lord Denning stated that not only were "major mental diseases . . . such as schizophrenia . . . clearly diseases of the mind" but so too were disorders falling within the definition given in the key principle above. [1963] A.C. 386

Commentary
This definition was doubted in *Quick* (see below) and in *R. v Burgess* (1991) (see p.153) where it was said that a disease of the mind could exist even without a danger of recurrence. A disease of the mind can also exist without a violent manifestation.

Key Principle: **To amount to a disease of the mind, the cause of the malfunctioning of the mind must be something other than an external factor of transitory effect.**

R. v Quick & Paddison 1973
A diabetic nurse assaulted a patient during what might have been a hypoglycaemic lapse of consciousness caused by consuming alcohol and failing to eat after taking insulin. He pleaded guilty after the judge ruled that his defence, if any, amounted to insanity.

Held: (CA) Defendant's appeal allowed. Any malfunction of his mind was not caused by "a bodily disorder" such as the diabetes. It was caused by external factors (using insulin, drinking and failing to eat regularly) and so did not amount to insanity. "A malfunctioning of the mind of transitory effect caused by the application to the body of some external factor . . . cannot fairly be said to be due to disease." [1973] Q.B. 910

Commentary
The appropriate defence was automatism. The court felt that the width of the definitions of disease of the mind given in *Kemp* and *Bratty v Attorney-General for Northern Ireland* (1963) (see above) might lead to unacceptable results if not restricted to internal factors. The dichotomy between internal and external cause have produced surprising results. In *R. v Sullivan* (1984) a man of

"blameless reputation" involuntarily caused grievous bodily harm by automatic movements during an epileptic seizure. Adopting *Kemp*, the House of Lords ruled that the defence was insanity because it did not matter whether the impairment was organic or functional, permanent, transitory or intermittent. The position would differ if the impairment had been the result of some external physical factor. Likewise, whilst the defendant diabetic in *Quick* was held to be a non-insane automaton during the hypoglycaemic attack, a diabetic in *R. v Hennessy* (1989) was held to be insane. In the former the condition was caused by external factors, whilst in the latter, hyperglycaemia was caused by failure to take insulin, stress and anxiety. Thus the Court of Appeal held that it had arisen, if at all, from internal factors (including the diabetes itself). Finally, in *R. v Burgess* (1991), a man attacked a friend, possibly whilst sleepwalking. Following *Sullivan*, the Court of Appeal held that this amounted to insanity because the cause was internal.

Key Principle: **Automatism requires proof of an involuntary act done whilst not conscious of one's actions.**

Bratty v Attorney-General for Northern Ireland 1963
(see p.151).

Held: (HL) Defendant's appeal dismissed for reasons given below. Lord Denning defined automatism as "an act done by the muscles without any control by the mind . . . or an act done by a person who is not conscious of what he is doing . . . an involuntary act . . .". [1963] A.C. 386

Commentary
Unlike the defence of insanity which leads to a special verdict, a finding of non-insane automatism leads to an acquittal.

Key Principle: **Not every unconscious, involuntary act amounts to non-insane automatism.**

Bratty v Attorney-General for Northern Ireland 1963
(see p.151).

Held: (HL) Appeal dismissed. The judge was correct not to leave automatism to the jury. The only apparent cause of the defendant's involuntary act was the psychomotor epilepsy (a disease of the mind within the *M'Naghten* rules). Therefore the defence was insanity not automatism. [1963] A.C. 386

Commentary

(1) Not only do insanity (internal cause see *Sullivan*) and automatism (external cause see *Quick*) differ in outcome, they also differ in burden of proof. As stated in *Bratty*, the burden of proving insanity is on the defence but the burden of disproving automatism is on the prosecution. The case also establishes that where the defence raises automatism, the prosecution (or judge) may introduce insanity.

(2) Involuntary act arising from intoxication is governed by the rules on intoxication and an act is not involuntary just because it is unintended or the result of irresistible impulse: *Bratty*. Examples of non-insane automatism given in the case were reflex actions, convulsions, lack of consciousness caused by a blow on the head, concussion, and sleepwalking. This last example is now incorrect following *Burgess* (see p.153). A further example of automatism given in *Quick* and *Sullivan* was that of actions occurring whilst recovering from an anaesthetic. Moreover, in *R. v T* (1990), the Crown Court held that automatism might be a defence when post traumatic stress disorder was induced by a rape (an external factor).

Key Principle: **Self-induced automatism may be a defence to a crime of specific intent but not to one of basic intent if the defendant was reckless in becoming an automaton.**

R. v Bailey 1983

The defendant was convicted of wounding with intent. He claimed to have been in a state of automatism caused by hypoglycaemia. He appealed against the direction that self-induced automatism was no defence.

Held: (CA) Appeal dismissed. Despite the misdirection there was no miscarriage of justice. Applying the reasoning from

Majewski, self-induced automatism could provide a defence to crimes of specific intent. Moreover, not every self-induced automaton would be reckless in the sense envisaged in *Majewski*. It is not common knowledge, even amongst diabetics, that the consequence of failing to eat after taking insulin can be "aggressive, unpredictable and uncontrollable conduct". Therefore, self-induced automatism (arising from factors other than drink or drugs) may be a defence to a basic intent crime unless the prosecution prove that the defendant was reckless in the sense of realising this likely effect of the action or inaction. [1983] 2 All E.R. 503

Commentary
In *Quick*, the Court of Appeal stated that self-induced or reasonably foreseeable incapacity would not excuse. The court in *Bailey* viewed this as *obiter*. In any event, *Quick* was decided before *Majewski* and *Bailey* brings the law on self-induced automatism into line with that now applicable to self-induced intoxication (see *Hardie*).

---

14. DEFENCES (2)

Duress

Key Principle: **The defendant's will must be overborne by a threat of death or serious personal injury.**

R. v Valderrama-Vega 1985
The defendant pleaded duress to a charge of importing drugs. The defence was based on his severe financial hardship; threats of injury to himself and his family; and threats to expose his homosexuality. He was convicted on a direction that duress was only a defence if he acted "solely" because of the threats of death or serious injury.

Held: (CA) Defendant's appeal dismissed. Threats of death or serious injury did not have to be the sole cause of the defendant's behaviour but only threats of that nature could amount to duress. In the context of the direction as a whole, the jury had not been misled. [1985] Crim. L.R. 220

Commentary
The threat need not be against the defendant. As this case illustrates, threats against one's family are also sufficient.

Key Principle: **The threat must be present and immediate, placing the defendant in an unavoidable dilemma.**

R. v Hudson & Taylor 1971
The defendants committed perjury, having been threatened with violence if they did not do so. They pleaded duress but were convicted on a direction that, the threat was not present and immediate at the time of the crime because it could only be carried out in the future.

Held: (CA) Defendant's appeal allowed. Whilst the threat must be present and immediate, the injury threatened need not be capable of being carried out immediately. Moreover, whilst the defence may be lost by a failure to take the opportunity to render the threat ineffective, regard must be given to whether such an opportunity is reasonably open to the defendant, taking into account age, circumstances and any risks involved in trying to do so. [1971] 2 Q.B. 202

Commentary
The court also indicated that one factor to consider was how effective (or ineffective) police protection might be. On the issue of immediacy, compare two analogous cases dealing with duress of circumstances: *R. v Cole* (1994) (see p.157) and *R. v Abdul-Hussain* (1999) (see p.161).

Key Principle: **The defence cannot be used where defendants voluntarily place themselves in a situation which they know might give rise to duress.**

R. v Sharp 1987
The defendant voluntarily joined a gang of robbers, knowing of the leader's propensity for violence. When he tried to withdraw, the leader threatened to kill him. The defendant was convicted of manslaughter in the course of a robbery and appealed on the basis that duress should have been left to the jury.

Held: (CA) Appeal dismissed. Duress is not available where the defendant voluntarily joins an organisation as an active member, knowing of its nature and knowing that pressure might be used to persuade him to maintain his involvement. [1987] Q.B. 853

R. v Shepherd 1988
The defendant voluntarily joined a gang of thieves. When he tried to withdraw, he was threatened by a member of the gang who had several previous convictions including offences of violence. The defendant raised duress in defence to offences committed thereafter but was convicted after the judge withdrew the defence because of his voluntary association with the gang.

Held: (CA) Defendant's appeal allowed. Where the risk of duress is freely undertaken there is no defence but the position differs where the group or member's propensity for violence was not known. The jury had not been given the opportunity to consider this point. (1988) 86 Cr.App.R. 47

Commentary
See also *R. v Ali* (1995) where the importance of knowledge of the violent nature of the enterprise or persons involved was stressed in denying the defence to a heroin addict who committed robbery to pay debts to his supplier whom he knew to have a reputation for violence. There had been some conflict in this area following the Court of Appeal decisions in *R. v Baker & Ward* (1999), *R. v Heath* (2000) and *R. v Harmer* (2002). In *R. v Z* (2003) the Court of Appeal chose to follow *R. v Baker & Ward*. The court decided that voluntary association with criminals was only relevant if the defendant could anticipate pressure from them to commit a crime of the same type (*i.e.* seriousness) as the one committed.

Key Principle: **Duress is only available if the crime committed is one that the defendant was instructed, under threat, to commit.**

R. v Cole 1994
The defendant committed two robberies to repay debts to persons who had threatened him, his girlfriend and their child with violence if the debts were not repaid.

Held: (CA) Defendant's appeal dismissed in respect of duress. The defence was limited to cases where the threatener "nominates" the crime and the moneylenders had not stipulated that the defendant should commit robbery. [1994] Crim. L.R. 582

Commentary
Whilst the threatener must nominate the crime, this may be done in general terms as in *Ali* (above) where the supplier had similarly threatened violence if debts were not repaid but had also handed the defendant a gun and told him to get the money from a building society or bank by the next day.

Key Principle: **The defendant must respond to the threat as would a sober person of reasonable firmness, sharing the defendant's relevant characteristics.**

R. v Graham 1982
The defendant was convicted of murdering his wife and pleaded duress based on a belief that his lover would kill him if he did not do so. He appealed against the direction that the test for establishing duress was objective.

Held: (CA) Appeal dismissed. The defence is limited by an objective test which was "would a sober person of reasonable firmness, sharing the characteristics of the defendant . . . have so responded". [1982] 1 W.L.R. 294

Commentary
This test is similar to that previously used in provocation under *DPP v Camplin* (1978) (see Ch.6) and was confirmed in *R. v Howe* (1987) (see p.159). It may be that in the future the courts will now adopt the test laid down in *R. v Smith* (2001) (see Ch.6). As in provocation, voluntary intoxication is not taken into account in applying the test. Nor is a self-induced drug addiction (*R. v Flatt* (1996)) or low IQ (*R. v Bowen* (1996)) because neither are relevant, as such, to the ability to withstand threats. Nor are characteristics such as "unusual pliability or vulnerability to pressure" (*R. v Horne* (1994)) or "emotional instability (and) neurotic states" (*R. v Hegarty* (1994)) since these conflict with the requirement of "reasonable firmness".

Key Principle: **If the defendant makes a mistake about the**

existence of duress, s/he may be entitled to be judged on the facts as s/he believed them to be.

R. v Safi 2003

The defendants pleaded duress to the charge of a number of offences involved in hijacking a plane. They were convicted and appealed against the judge's direction that they could not rely on a mistaken belief that there was an imminent peril.

Held: (CA) Appeal allowed. It was not necessary that there was, in fact, an imminent peril. A defendant was entitled to rely on a belief in the existence of a threat. [2003] Crim. L.R. 721

Commentary

This confirms the decision in *R. v Cairns* (1999). The court also suggested that a defendant could only rely on a mistaken belief in duress if that mistake was based on reasonable grounds. This was also the view of the Court of Appeal, *obiter*, in *R. v Graham* (1982) (see p.158) (approved, *obiter*, by the House of Lords in *R. v Howe* (1987) (below)). On the other hand, the Court of Appeal in *R. v Martin* (2000) decided that self-defence and duress were analogous and that mistaken belief in duress did not have to be based on reasonable grounds.

Key Principle: **Duress is no defence to murder.**

R. v Howe 1987

The defendant and others were convicted of, *inter alia*, murder and appealed on three points. One raised the issue of the objective test in duress (referred to above), another raised the issue of liability of accomplices (Ch.12) and another was whether duress was available as a defence to a principal offender to murder.

Held: (HL) Appeal dismissed. Duress was no defence to murder as an accomplice or principal offender. *Lynch* (1975) was overruled and *Abbott* (1977) affirmed. [1987] A.C. 417

Commentary

According to *Lynch* duress was a defence for an accomplice to murder but, according to *Abbott* (PC), it was no defence to the principal offender. In *Howe*, the House decided that no rational distinction could be drawn in terms of degrees of participation. Basing the decision on a number of grounds, including morality and policy, the House then followed *Abbott* and overruled *Lynch*. The court noted that their decision could lead to anomalies. Not least was the fact that duress might still be a defence to attempted murder and *Offences Against the Person Act 1861*, s.18 where the *mens rea* requirement was satisfied by the same level of blameworthiness as for murder and where the victim's survival could be by coincidence rather than design. Two of their Lordships suggested that the defence could also be excluded in cases of attempted murder. This was applied in the next case.

Key Principle: **Duress is no defence to attempted murder.**

R. v Gotts 1992
The defendant unsuccessfully raised duress as a defence to attempted murder.

Held: (HL) Appeal dismissed. There was no justification in logic, morals or law for a distinguishing between a successful and would-be murderer. [1992] 2 A.C. 412

Commentary
Whilst the "sanctity of life" could not justify the exclusion of the defence from attempted as opposed to successful murder, the court was swayed by the fact that the mens rea of the offence required more "evil" intent than that for murder.

Necessity (Duress of Circumstances)

Key Principle: **Duress of circumstances may be available as a defence where the defendant's action arises from a fear of death or serious injury.**

R. v Conway 1989
The defendant claimed that he drove recklessly because he thought that two men approaching his car intended to kill his passenger. He was convicted and appealed on the basis that necessity (acting in an emergency to save his passenger) was a defence.

Held: (CA) Appeal allowed. Necessity could be a defence where it amounted to duress of circumstances (*i.e.* where circumstances constrained the defendant to act to avoid death or serious injury to himself or another). [1989] Q.B. 290

Commentary

The defence was not "pure" duress because the crime committed was not nominated by the threatener. However, the court accepted the argument from *Howe* that duress was a species of necessity. Whilst there might not be a general defence of necessity, in these circumstances the defence might be available subject to the same limitations as those imposed on the defence of duress. The defence does not therefore extend to fear of psychological damage: *R. v Baker & Wilkins* (1997) (see p.167).

Key Principle: **There must be a present and immediate peril to which the defendant responds.**

R. v Abdul-Hussain et al 1999

The defendants hijacked an aeroplane in order to escape death at the hands of the Iraqi authorities. They appealed against conviction based on a direction that the threat was insufficiently close and immediate.

Held: (CA) Appeal allowed. Imminent peril of death or serious injury to the defendant or their dependants must be operating to overbear the defendant's will at the time of the offence. The threatened injury need not be immediate. [1999] Crim. L.R. 570

Commentary

(1) The test is similar to that in *Hudson & Taylor* on duress. For examples where the defence was lost due to lack of immediacy see *R. v Cole* 1994 (see p.157) where the link between the peril and the offences was not direct and immediate and *Blake v DPP* (1993) (Ch.10, p.114) where the vicar was denied the defence of duress of circumstances because writing on the pillar was not in response to fear of immediate danger to himself or those with him.

(2) The Court of Appeal confirmed the view expressed in *R. v Pommell* (see p.162) that the defence extends to all crimes except murder, attempted murder and treason. However,

this should be considered in the light of *Re A (children)* (2000) (see p.163).

Key Principle: **The circumstances must be such that a person of reasonable firmness, sharing the defendant's characteristics, would respond as the defendant did.**

R. v Martin 1989
The defendant drove his stepson to work whilst disqualified and pleaded necessity based on a threat from his wife (who had a history of suicidal behaviour) that she would kill herself if he did not do so. He appealed against the direction that necessity was no defence.

Held: (CA) Appeal allowed. The defence was only available if "from an objective standpoint" the defendant acted "reasonably and proportionately" to avoid a threat of death or serious injury. The jury should therefore have decided whether or not a sober person of reasonable firmness, sharing the defendant's characteristics, would have responded similarly. [1989] 1 All E.R. 652

Commentary

(1) The test is the same as for duress and is confirmed in *R. v Abdul-Hussain* (1999) (above). *Abdul-Hussain* indicates that the court should look at all the circumstances in deciding whether the defendant's response to the peril was reasonable and proportionate. These would include the type of peril, the numbers involved, the identity and status of those creating the peril, the opportunity available to avoid the peril and any time lapse between the peril and the offence. The defendant must desist from the crime as soon as reasonably possible after the peril ceases to be present. Thus in *DPP v Bell* (1992) the defence succeeded where the defendant drove whilst intoxicated in order to escape from a threat of violence because he only drove a short way until a safe distance from his pursuers. Contrast *R. v Tomkinson* (2001) where the defence was lost because the intoxicated defendant drove 72 miles from the danger before being arrested. Also in *R. v Pommell* (1995), it was for the jury to

decide whether the defendant, who took possession of a firearm to prevent another from using it, had acted as soon as reasonable in the circumstances when he failed to hand it over to the police immediately.

(2) *R. v Martin* also establishes that any mistaken belief must be based on reasonable grounds. However this should be contrasted with the view expressed in *R. v Martin* (2000) (see p.159) that the test should be subjective as in duress. Also see *DPP v Rogers* (1998) which also suggests a subjective test.

Key Principle: **Necessity is no defence to murder except in highly exceptional circumstances.**

R. v Dudley & Stephens 1884
The defendants and victim were shipwrecked on a boat, 1000 miles from land. After nine days without food and seven without water, the defendants killed and ate the victim in order to save themselves. If they had not done so they would probably have died and that the victim, being the youngest and weakest, was likely to have died before them. The defendants were charged with murder.

Held: (DC) Conviction affirmed. There was no authority that necessity (other than self-defence) justified a killing. Saving life by killing an innocent and unoffending victim did not fall within the scope of any defence known to the law. [1884] 14 Q.B.D. 273

Commentary
The case suggests that it was not in fact necessary to kill the boy. However it appears to go further in holding that it would not, in any event, have been a defence. *Dudley & Stephens* is distinguished in the next case.

Re A (children) (conjoined twins: surgical separation) 2000
Doctors wished to operate to separate conjoined twins, Jodie and Mary. Jodie was capable of independent existence but the operation would kill Mary who was alive only because she was joined to Jodie. Without the operation both twins would die. The judge concluded that the operation would be lawful and the parents appealed.

Held: (CA) Appeal dismissed. The operation would be lawful because, *per* Brooke L.J., "According to Sir James Stephen" (*Digest of Criminal Law*, 1887), "there are three necessary requirements for the application of the doctrine of necessity:

(i) the act is needed to avoid inevitable and irreparable evil;

(ii) no more should be done than is reasonably necessary for the purpose to be achieved; and

(iii) the evil inflicted must not be disproportionate to the evil avoided.

. . . I consider that all three of these requirements are satisfied in this case."

Commentary
Lord Brooke felt that *Dudley & Stephens* could be distinguished because there was no issue about how to select the victim in this case and because Mary (unlike the cabin boy in Dudley) was a threat to Jodie. His decision is also limited by the fact that the victim was already "designated for death". Lord Walker dismissed the appeal on other grounds and Lord Ward limited his decision to cases where doctors had to choose between two conflicting duties towards patients. Therefore it is unlikely that the case provides any general precedent in cases of murder.

Self-defence and Prevention of Crime

Key Principle: **A person is entitled to use reasonable force, at common law, in defence of themselves or another and also, under *Criminal Law Act 1967*, s.3 to prevent a crime or effect an arrest.**

Key Principle: **Whilst the circumstances giving rise to a plea under s.3 or at common law may differ, they also overlap and the legal requirements for both are similar.**

R. v Clegg 1995
A soldier shot and killed a car passenger and was convicted of murder following an unsuccessful plea of self-defence. The first three shots fired were, he claimed, in defence of himself or a

fellow soldier. The fourth shot was fired after the perceived danger had passed and so, if anything, could only fall within the Northern Ireland equivalent of s.3 (force used to effect an arrest). In the circumstances the use of lethal force was excessive and unreasonable. One question on appeal was whether any distinction could be drawn between excessive force used in self-defence and that used in prevention of crime or to effect arrest.

Held: (HL) Defendant's appeal dismissed for reasons given below. It was not practical to distinguish between the defences because of the potential overlap between them. The degree of permissible force and the consequence of using excessive force was the same in each defence, irrespective of whether the defendant is a civilian, a member of the security forces or a police officer. [1995] 1 A.C. 482

Commentary

It is not only the concept of reasonable force that is the same for both defences. The effect of the defences and the law relating to mistaken belief in the need to use force is also the same. Moreover, the burden of proof is on the prosecution in respect of the common law defence (*Palmer v R.* (1971) (see p.167)) and s.3 (*R. v Kahn* (1995)). *Clegg* also illustrates that reasonable force can be used, at common law, to defend another (and oneself). It may also be used to defend property (for example *Scarlett* (see p.168) and *Attorney-General's Reference (No.2 of 1983)* (1984) (see below)).

Key Principle: **For defensive force to be reasonable, it must be necessary to use the force in response to an attack or the fear of an imminent attack.**

Attorney-General's Reference (No.2 of 1983) 1984

The defendant was charged with, *inter alia,* having made an explosive substance (petrol bombs). He was acquitted on the basis of self-defence in that he intended to use the bombs to protect his premises from what he feared to be an imminent attack from rioters and looters.

Held: (CA) The use of reasonable force was not limited to spontaneous reactions on being attacked. It also covered acts done in anticipation of imminent danger and could, therefore, provide a lawful excuse in such cases. [1984] Q.B. 456

Key Principle: **It may still be necessary to use force even though the defendant has not retreated or demonstrated a willingness to disengage before resorting to force.**

R. v McInnes 1971

The defendant stabbed and killed the victim during a fight. He appealed against conviction for murder based on, *inter alia*, the direction that self-defence is only available if the defendant has done all he reasonably can to retreat before using force.

Held: (CA) Appeal dismissed. Although the direction was too rigid, it had not misled the jury. A failure to retreat is not conclusive, it is simply one factor to take into account in deciding whether or not it was necessary to use force. [1971] 1 W.L.R. 1600

Commentary

The court approved *R. v Julien* (1969) which stated that there was no duty to retreat but that there was a duty to demonstrate an unwillingness to fight. This latter condition was held to be too stringent in the next case.

R. v Bird 1985

The defendant was convicted of wounding. Her evidence was that, at the time, she was being held by the victim against a wall and struck back at him in self-defence. She appealed against the direction that it was necessary that she demonstrated an unwillingness to fight before striking.

Held: (CA) Appeal allowed. Failing to demonstrate willingness to disengage was, like failure to retreat, not conclusive but simply one factor to take into account along with the rest of the evidence. [1985] 2 All E.R. 513

Commentary

The court agreed that failing to retreat or to offer to withdraw might establish retaliation, revenge or pure aggression rather than self-defence. However, this would not always be the case.

Key Principle: **If the defendant genuinely but mistakenly believed that it was necessary to use force, s/he is entitled to be judged on the facts as s/he believed them to be.**

Beckford v R. 1988
An armed police officer was convicted of murder, having shot and killed the victim. He appealed against the direction that he could only rely on his mistaken belief that he was acting in self-defence if it was based on reasonable grounds.

Held: (PC) Appeal allowed. Following *Williams (Gladstone)* a genuine belief that it was necessary to use force would negate the intent to act unlawfully. Therefore the test for self-defence is whether the force is reasonable in the circumstances as the defendant honestly believed them to be. The belief does not also have to be reasonable. [1988] A.C. 130

Commentary
The same principle applies to *Criminal Law Act 1967*, s.3: *R. v Baker & Wilkins* (1997). In this case the defendant and her co-defendant were convicted of criminal damage, having broken through a door to gain access to her child who was being hidden by its father. Although the defendants were entitled to be judged on their honest belief, their appeal was dismissed because even so no crime was being committed and so there was no right to use force. Their defence based on *Criminal Damage Act 1971*, s.5(2)(b) (see p.115) and on duress of circumstances (see p.161) also failed.

Key Principle: **The degree of force used must be proportionate and no more than necessary in the circumstances.**

Palmer v R. 1971
The defendant was convicted of murder, having shot and killed the victim, in what he claimed to be self-defence.

Held: (PC) Defendant's appeal dismissed for reasons given below. The defence only applied where force was reasonably necessary. This depended on the circumstances of the case but a jury should bear in mind that "a person defending himself cannot weigh to a nicety the exact measure of his necessary defensive action." [1971] A.C. 814

Commentary

Consider also *McInnes* where the deliberate stabbing was unreasonable in the circumstances and *Clegg* where the use of lethal force against someone not believed to be involved in terrorist activities was "grossly disproportionate to the mischief to be averted". The court in *Palmer* commented that doing what one "honestly and instinctively" thought was necessary was, at most, strong evidence that the force used was reasonable. Despite apparent doubts caused by the later case of *Scarlett* (see below), it is clear that the test for the degree of permissible force is objective. This is confirmed in *R. v Martin* (2002) where the defendant shot two burglars, killing one and wounding the other. He suffered from a paranoid personality disorder that caused him to believe he was in extreme peril. The Court of Appeal distinguished *R. v Smith* (2001) (see p.62) on provocation and held that the psychiatric disorder was not relevant in assessing the use of reasonable force in self-defence. This should be contrasted with the decision in *R. v Martin* (2000) (see p.159) and compared with the next key principle.

Key Principle: **If the defendant makes a mistake about the circumstances in which force is used, s/he is entitled to be judged on the facts as s/he believed them to be in determining whether, objectively, the force used was reasonable.**

R. v Scarlett 1993

A pub landlord was convicted of constructive manslaughter based on an act of assault. He appealed on the ground that the act causing death was an exercise of reasonable force used to eject a trespasser from the pub.

Held: (CA) Appeal allowed. Even an unreasonable mistaken belief that force used was lawful precluded the *mens rea* of assault: *Williams* and *Beckford*. Therefore the defendant could only be convicted if the degree of force used was excessive in the circumstances as he honestly believed them to be. [1993] 4 All E.R. 629

Commentary

The court decided that there was no distinction between mistakes relating to necessity (*Williams* and *Beckford*) and those relating to the degree of force needed (the instant case). The decision caused consternation because of a suggestion that the test for reasonable force was also subjective (*i.e.* that the defendant was entitled to use the degree of force that s/he believed was reasonable). However, it is clear that this is not correct. The force used must be objectively reasonable in the light of the facts (including the circumstances and the danger) as the defendant, subjectively, believed them to be: *Shaw (Norman) v R.* (2001).

Key Principle: **A successful (or unsuccessful) plea under s.3 or at common law does not mitigate: it is either a complete defence or no defence at all.**

R. v Clegg 1995

(see p.164). The first question raised by the appeal was whether a verdict of manslaughter, rather than murder, was available where self-defence failed because the force used was excessive.

Held: (HL) If the defence succeeds it leads to an acquittal. If it fails it leads to a finding of guilty as charged. Therefore the defendant was guilty of murder because an unsuccessful plea did not mitigate the crime to manslaughter. [1995] 1 A.C. 482

Commentary

The court expressed the same view that led to convictions for murder in *Palmer* and *McInnes*. Regret was expressed and various recommendations for reform were considered but, ultimately, the House held that any change must be by Parliament and not the courts.

INDEX

This index has been prepared using Sweet and Maxwell's Legal Taxonomy. Main index entries conform to keywords provided by the Legal Taxonomy except where references to specific documents or non-standard terms (denoted by quotation marks) have been included. These keywords provide a means of identifying similar concepts in other Sweet & Maxwell publications and online services to which keywords from the Legal Taxonomy have been applied. Readers may find some minor differences between terms used in the text and those which appear in the index. Suggestions to *taxonomy@sweetandmaxwell.co.uk*.

(All references are to page number)